English ⌗ Heritage
Book of

Wharram Percy
Deserted Medieval Village

English ⌗ Heritage
Book of
Wharram Percy
Deserted Medieval Village

Maurice Beresford
and
John Hurst

B. T. Batsford Ltd/ English Heritage
London

ISBN 0 7134 6113 6 (cased)
ISBN 0 7134 6114 4 (limp)

Typeset by Lasertext, Stretford, Manchester
and printed in Great Britain by
The Bath Press, Bath
for the publishers
B. T. Batsford Ltd
4 Fitzhardinge Street
London W1H 0AH

2004 003 934

Contents

List of illustrations

List of colour plates

Acknowledgements

Although two names appear on the title page of this book and the responsibility for the views in it are theirs, the 40 years' researches described in it would have been impossible without the help, at different times, of many others, often unpaid volunteers. Among these are:

The site owners, the late 11th Baron Middleton, the 12th Baron Middleton and the farm tenants, the Midgley family, for permission to excavate and for their continued help and interest over the years; the church authorities in the 1960s when the Faculty to excavate was granted; the Milner family who for the 40 years of the project have provided local help and support.

John Hurst has directed the Wharram Research project since 1953. Since 1950 Professor Maurice Beresford was responsible for recruiting volunteers from Universities, schools, a Borstal, an Approved School and the general public. Until recently he also organized food supplies and public relations, and was responsible for the accounts.

The excavations of some 100 sites within the village area have been supervised by many different people. Full lists of the unpaid volunteers who worked at the peasant house sites 10 and 6 and at the church are given in the monographs (see p. 132) but particular mention should be made of Dr Robin Glasscock, Mrs Betty Ewins, Mrs Jean Le Patourel and Miss Christine Mahany. The 1970s and 1980s excavations sponsored by the Department of the Environment and English Heritage were supervised by the following: the watermill and fishpond, Dr Colin Treen and Malcolm Atkin; the boundaries, Mike McCarthy, Richard Daggett and Paul Herbert; the north manor, Gustav Milne, Professor Philip Rahtz, Dr Steven Roskams and Dr Julian Richards; Toft 10, Dr Paul Stamper and Robert Croft; the post-medieval and medieval parsonages, Miss Charlotte Harding and John Wood; and the Improv-ing farm, Dr Stuart Wrathmell and Alex Gilmour. Richard Porter has directed site survey since 1955.

Since 1974 the parishes research project has been directed by Dr Colin Hayfield. Professor Kenneth St Joseph, of the Cambridge Committee for Aerial Photography, has taken an important series of photographs of the village from 1948, and Tony Pacitto of the general area during the 1970s and 1980s. The excavated sites have been marked out for display to the visitor under the supervision of Warwick Burton and Richard Coulton. Dr Richard Gulliver has supervised the ecological management and Dr Colin Treen the landscaping. Special thanks are due to the York office of English Heritage for their help over the years.

Many hundreds of volunteers from many parts of the world have assisted the actual excavation or helped in many other ways. Mrs Joan Summerson has, over 30 years, provided a lifeline to the outside world by shopping for the project.

The current publications are under the general editorship of Dr Stuart Wrathmell, and the finds and general post-excavation work are co-ordinated by Mrs Ann Clark. Special thanks are due to the work of the Ancient Monuments Laboratory and Drawing Office.

The sources of the historical documentation lie principally in the Public Record Office and the British Library, London; the Borthwick Institute of Historical Research, University of York; the Dean and Chapter Library, York; the County Record Offices for North Yorkshire and for Humberside; Nottingham University Library (Middleton MSS); Reading University Library (Englefield MSS); and Castle Howard (Dacre Survey). The help of the archivists is acknowledged. We have also had access to maps and documents in the estate offices at Sledmere and Birdsall and to material from the Halifax (Garrowby) estate in the custody of Dibb and Clegg, solicitors, Barnsley, seen by courtesy of Mr Buckley. To these historical researches, extending over many years, Dr Keith Allison, Dr Barbara English, Dr Colin Hayfield and Richard Porter have rendered generous assistance.

All the illustrations are the copyright of the Wharram Research Project except for the following:

Ancient Monuments Laboratory, 61 and colour plate 5

Birdsall Estate Office, 69

Borthwick Institute of Historical Research of the University of York, 80, 83

British Academy Corpus of Anglo-Saxon Stone Sculpture, 62

University of Cambridge Committee for Aerial Photography, 4, 25, 32, 59, 92, colour plate 3. Cambridge University Collection: Copyright reserved.

Simon Clark, 50 and front cover

Myrtle Milner, 13

Ministry of Defence, 5, 6, 7, 70. Reproduced by permission of the Controller of HMSO

North Yorkshire County Record Office: 84, 85

Tony Pacitto, 51, 66

Public Record Office, 16, 30, 75. Crown Copyright reproduced by permission of the Controller of Her Majesty's Stationery Office

Royal Commission on the Historical Monuments of England, 9, 10, 36a and b and colour plate 1

John Rylands University Library of Manchester, 73. Reproduced by courtesy of the Director and University Librarian

Andrew Selkirk, 18

Special thanks are due to Peter Dunn of the Ancient Monuments Drawing Office, English Heritage, for his reconstruction drawings, 8, 28, 76, 78 and colour plates 2, 9, 13 and his redrawing or updating of many of the figures. Other drawings were redrawn or updated by Chris Philo.

J. G. Hurst
M. W. Beresford

Introduction

The explorations chronicled in this volume, which have now extended over 40 years, began very simply and almost by accident in 1948. They were at first wholly centred on two grass fields of extensive earthworks near a semi-abandoned ancient parish church but eventually developed into a study of the changes that the whole local landscape had undergone in past centuries. At that time such earthworks, the remains of houses and streets from an abandoned medieval village, had received very little attention from either archaeologists or historians. At Wharram Percy a partnership began between an historian and an archaeologist, the authors of this book, that eventually expanded to become a major research project involving many specialists from diverse disciplines. This work was helped over the years by several hundred volunteers of all ages and from many countries.

Archaeology, in the popular sense of excavations, began at Wharram Percy in 1950, just about the time when 'medieval archaeology' was first emerging as a serious study: the first annual issue of a journal, *Medieval Archaeology*, appeared in 1957, following the foundation of the Society for Medieval Archaeology. Previously archaeology had been concerned mainly with periods of history before written documents and from which few structures had survived entire. In so far as medieval buildings had been excavated, they were castles and monasteries not farms and domestic houses of a village, and often the excavators had no interest other than the recovery of a ground plan for the building in its latest phase just before its abandonment or destruction.

Contrary to common belief, there are very few houses of the medieval English village below the status of the manor house that are still standing in the north of England: the picturesque cottages of calendars, posters and travel brochures are usually from the sixteenth century or later. Obviously archaeologists could not excavate below houses and cottages in existing villages to seek for medieval houses, but an abandoned site was attractive since it had no such restrictions.

Thus the first excavations at Wharram Percy – as at other sites inspired by them – were concerned to recover the plans of the late-medieval houses that lay immediately below the surface – and to contrast the surroundings in which a peasant lived with those of lords in their manor houses and castles. Medieval archaeology, however, soon became involved with the remains of houses of earlier periods, lying at deeper levels, and thus with the whole sequence of occupation, eventually going back to the prehistoric.

Once appropriate techniques had been developed, medieval archaeology was able to extend to explore other sequences of this sort that were concealed under the standing remains of larger buildings, such as manor houses and churches. Here again, the best opportunities lay on sites like Wharram Percy whose manor houses had been long abandoned and whose parish church had fallen into disuse.

In the same years after the Second World War a subject, post-medieval archaeology – also with its relevant journal – appeared on the scene, and Chapters 3–6 of this book show that excavations within the church and at the site of the vicarage and an adjoining farmhouse were able to extend the sequences of occupation forward from the middle ages. Indeed they reached the twentieth century when, in the later seasons, the more extensive excavations in the valley were forced to uncover ground that in the first seasons had been used as cess and rubbish pits. Here was an unintended opportunity to study what 40 years in the soil had done to baked bean tins and corned beef cans.

Archaeology, whether medieval or post-medieval, is not confined to excavation. The results of 40 years' work described here have been achieved by incorporating excavation with the study of soil- and crop-marks in air photographs and with field-walking in search of pottery. At every stage the complementary evidence from documentary history, architectural history and oral history has been pursued. Correspondingly, the area of enquiry has extended to all five townships of Wharram Percy parish – once known simply as Lesser Wharram – and beyond to its neighbour, not deserted, the village that was once Greater Wharram but is now known as Wharram le Street.

As a result the village has been given a new life, for its name is known in archaeological circles world-wide. The work there has helped to transform our knowledge of the different forms that human settlement in the English countryside has taken at various times, making the history of the English village one of continual change.

The book aims to give the general reader an account of the progress of research up to the end of the July 1989 season of excavations. An historical narrative can proceed century by century from the remote past to the present day, but archaeology moves backwards in time, beginning with whatever period's remains are encountered immediately beneath the surface. In a complex site like Wharram Percy, with a long occupation, excavations have sometimes had to jump sideways through time from period to period, since the sub-surface remains at different parts of the site come from different periods. Sometimes they are the buildings of the village's predecessors, and sometimes of its successors.

Thus the order of the chapters is not a straightforward history of the village but an 'exploration', following the order in which discoveries were made. In doing so, they emphasize how interpretations of the archaeological evidence have necessarily changed and also how incomplete – and sometimes ambiguous – it is, even when supplemented by documentary evidences. A brief view of the chronological development of the village will be found in Chapter 8.

The book will also help the visitor to interpret the site for himself. The church and earthworks are now in the care of English Heritage. Excavation is scheduled to cease in the summer of 1990 after which the programme of interpretative signs, already in progress, will be completed. Eileen Power once observed that the study of History could rarely match the anticipation and excitement of an unfinished excavation. After 40 years the excavation of Wharram Percy has ceased but it is certainly unfinished: only about 6 per cent of the area within the English Heritage boundary fence has yet been excavated. There will now be a pause during the process of preparing the results for eventual full publication of data. After these have been digested, debated, and doubtlessly reinterpreted, future generations may wish to return to seek answers for questions that will seem as important to them as those that attracted an historian and an archaeologist to the site 40 years ago.

The site is attractively set in a lonely valley, with scenery and wild life characteristic of the high chalkland of the Yorkshire Wolds. A short walk-round guide, *Revealing Lost Villages: Wharram Percy*, published by English Heritage, is available at the nearest shop, which is the Post Office in Wharram le Street, and also at nearby English Heritage sites. At these, in a compact area of Yorkshire, the visitor can see several different levels of medieval life as represented by castles (Pickering, Helmsley and Scarborough), manor houses (Burton Agnes) and monastic sites (Kirkham, Byland and Rievaulx).

The public approach to the site (by a 550-yd/500-m footpath) is from a car-park situated on the south side of Bella Farm, which lies on a by-road to Burdale off the B1248 (Beverley–Malton) road. It is also signposted on the A166 (York–Bridlington) road. The site is open to the public throughout the year in hours of daylight.

1

The village site

No traveller comes easily to a lost village ...
You must be friend to mud, to green lanes
and unused footpaths, to rotting footbridges
and broken stiles, to brambles and to barbed
wire. It is a landscape that has forgotten that
human beings may want access, and it may
be pardoned for its forgetfulness. It is so long
since anyone wanted to come this way.

Maurice Beresford, *The Lost Villages of
England* (1954), p. 27.

The lost village

These words, written ruefully and with feeling
in 1952, were a distilled memory of nearly
a decade of field work in the Midlands and
Yorkshire. They were certainly applicable to a
sweltering day in June 1948 when a young
economic historian first made his way towards
the isolated parish church of St Martin,
Wharram Percy. The visit stimulated his own
researches and unconsciously set in motion the
40 years of collaborative and multi-disciplinary
work that is described in this book.

It was probably pride in being a finder that
led to the employment of the term '*lost* village'
for such sites, although it was soon to be
replaced with 'deserted', an adjective more
precise now that many village sites had in fact
been found, and one that echoed the title of
Oliver Goldsmith's poem, 'The Deserted Village', published in 1770. Goldsmith, writing of
a village depopulated in his own day, nevertheless encountered scepticism, writing to his
friend Sir Joshua Reynolds that '... some of my
friends think that the depopulation of villages
does not exist ... I have taken all possible pains
in my country excursions for these four or five
years past to be certain of what I allege.'

The village of Wharram Percy had been
deserted since the early sixteenth century, and
the last record of its villagers came in 1517
when a case was being prepared to prosecute
the landlord for the eviction of four families.

Unlike Goldsmith's Oxfordshire 'Auburn',
Wharram Percy had no poet to witness its
destruction, and there was much longer than
at Auburn for the memory of a village to pass
into oblivion, despite the survival of its parish
church as a reminder. In the intervening centuries the village houses decayed and grass came
to cover their foundations, the boundary walls
between farmyards and the streets themselves.
Three street names were incongruously preserved in the names of three fields that appeared
in seventeenth-century surveys of the church
glebe land as 'Water Lane', 'Towngate' and
'Town Street'.

Wharram Percy was not unique in this passage to oblivion. It is now known that nearly
3,000 medieval villages have failed to survive,
although until after 1945 it was a subject
that had barely entered the consciousness of
historians, geographers or archaeologists. Here
and there an antiquary or a local historian
drew a conclusion from an isolated or ruined
church, and occasionally some such folk myth
as a devasting plague, a destructive fire or
divine wrath was invoked to explain why village houses had disappeared from alongside a
church.

In the late fourteenth century the village of
Wharram Percy consisted of about 30 houses.
Like many others in the Yorkshire Wolds it
took the form of two facing Rows: the longer,
with about 20 houses, lay along the edge of a
hill-top plateau, faced by a shorter eastern row
on the valley floor, the two separated by the
steep fall of the valley side on which there seem
never to have been houses (**2**). The eviction of
four households that took place about 1500 may
have been the last stage in a depopulation
stretching over more than a century. Both the
former arable land of the village and its house
sites were then incorporated in a sheep run. In
the course of a tithe dispute in 1543 it was
claimed that 1,180 sheep (520 ewes, 340 wethers
and 300 hoggets) were kept at Wharram Percy

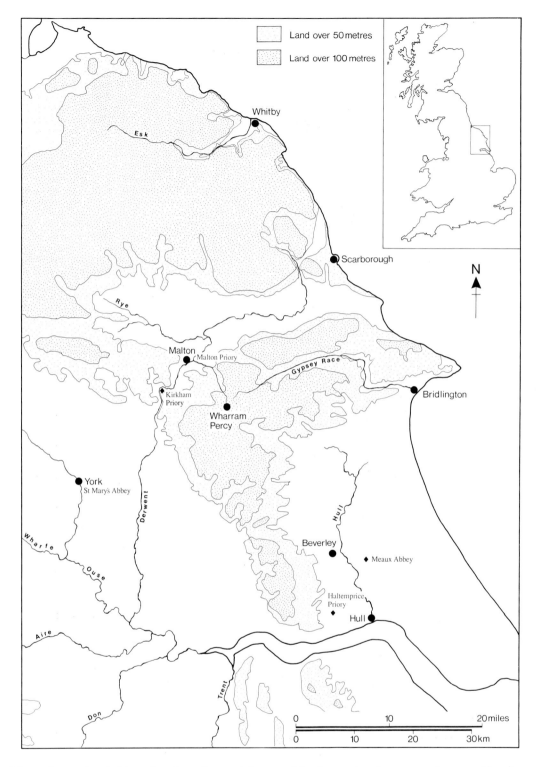

1 *Map of east Yorkshire showing the position of Wharram Percy in relation to the chalk Wolds,* *with the major towns and monastic sites mentioned in the text.*

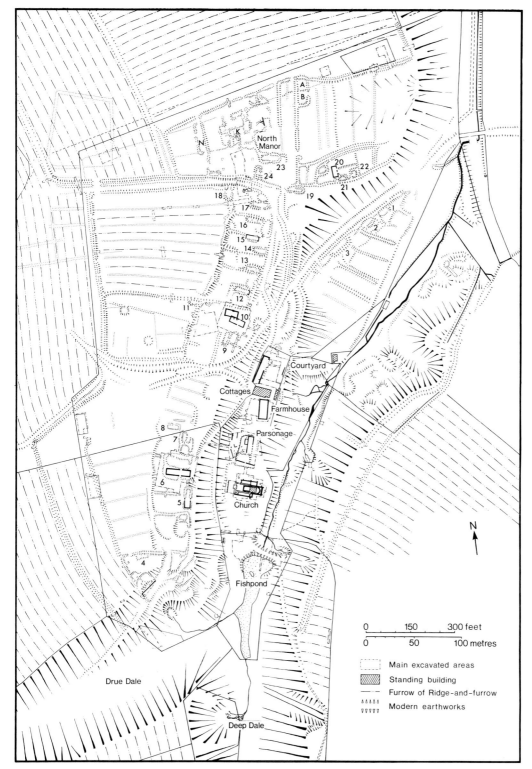

Labels on the plan:

North Manor

A
B
K
N
23
24
20
22
21
19
18
17
16
15
14
13
12
11
10
9
8
7
6
5
4
1
2
3
J

Courtyard
Cottages
Farmhouse
Parsonage
Church
Fishpond

Drue Dale
Deep Dale

N

| 0 | 150 | 300 feet |
| 0 | 50 | 100 metres |

Main excavated areas
Standing building
Furrow of Ridge-and-furrow
Modern earthworks

2 *Plan of the surviving earthworks of the medi-*
eval village of Wharram Percy showing the main
features referred to in the text.

pasture, then leased by a grazier from a village 10 miles (16 km) away.

The process of physical decay of the houses at the village site after the depopulation is not specifically documented, but the surface of the ground carried sufficient marks of buried foundations, and the former street levels were sufficiently indented, for their shapes to be recorded by those who were preparing the 6-in. (15-cm) Ordnance Survey in 1850–1, the first stage in the village's return from oblivion (3).

The surveyor's brief did not extend to recording history or archaeology, and it would seem to have been through the personal interest of the officer working in this area, Captain Bayly, that the Wharram Percy earthworks – and others in the High Wolds – were delineated on the Ordnance maps and named a 'village'. However, equally prominent village earthworks, in Yorkshire and beyond, remained unrecorded. When the large-scale Ordnance Survey plans were being revised in 1909 the officers of the Royal Engineers who were responsible sounded the views of East Yorkshire antiquarians and landowners: would it be safer to mark such earthwork as 'old foundations' or were they really the remains of villages? Opinion was divided, so 'villages' remained on the map. In 1850 there was no book, popular or

3 *First edition six-inch Ordnance Survey surveyed in 1850–1 and published in 1854. The main earthworks are visible and are correctly identified as the 'Site of the Village of Wharram Percy'.*

academic, on which the surveyor could have drawn to identify the earthworks as a village rather than as prehistoric or Roman settlements so that his reasons for his decision can only be conjectured. It was not necessarily the conjunction of the earthworks to a church that had suggested their identity, for similar earthworks on the Wolds without churches were also correctly identified as 'villages' (for example, Swaythorpe and Pockthorpe). Was there an oral tradition of former villages in the locality?

After the publication of the Ordnance map there was little further interest. By 1938 some deserted village sites had been identified by archaeologists (below, p. 31) although few of these were north of the Trent and none was in Yorkshire. They aroused no widespread interest in medieval settlement. Academic historians and historical geographers were no more active: as early as 1912 R. H. Tawney had published the plan of Whatborough, Leics., made in 1586, which showed 'the place where the towne [sc. village] of Whateboroughe stoode' but on the general issue he was cautious to the point of agnosticism: 'these isolated instances are worthless as a basis for generalisation'. Towards the end of his life, in conversation with Beresford and William Hoskins, he regretted that he had not sought out Whatborough on the ground: 'had I done so', he said, 'I would have left you two with nothing to do'.

In the autumn of 1938 Hoskins had stumbled on the site of Knaptoft, Leics., and subsequently took adult education classes from Leicester to this and other local sites, although his paper on the sites of the county did not appear until 1946.

The state of conventional wisdom is exemplified by the words of the doyen of economic historians, Professor Sir John Clapham, published posthumously in 1946: 'deserted villages are singularly rare in England ... there is very little evidence of [emptied villages] in Britain'. His editor, John Saltmarsh, added a more cautious footnote, for it was he who had drawn attention in 1943 to the evidence for widespread retreat of settlement on the Norfolk Breckland. By 1948 Clapham's view was untenable, for Hoskins had named some 60 Leicestershire sites, and Beresford, whose gazetteer for Warwickshire, with over 100 entries, was in the press, had begun researches that produced lists of many more in Northamptonshire, Buckinghamshire and Oxfordshire. It was clear from the proportions involved – from 10 to 13 per cent of villages in the central counties of the Midlands were deserted – that the causes of desertion were more than local.

The pioneering work by these economic historians was setting the Midland desertions in a context of general rural population decline in the later middle ages, with a substantial conversion of former arable to animal pasture. Because of the hostility of the law to depopulating enclosure after 1485, there was considerable documentary evidence from litigation to match the multitude of sites that now came to be recognized during field work on the ground.

The Tudor outcry against depopulation, the subject of Tawney's *Agrarian Problem in the Sixteenth Century*, had been centred on the Midland counties. As chance had it, this work by a number of scholars on the identification of deserted villages on the ground had begun

in the same area of England. It was less than certain, however, that the northern counties would prove a fruitful area for similar discoveries. Maurice Beresford took up a post at the University of Leeds in April 1948 and soon found that the North offered considerable scope to continue his work: a scrutiny of the first edition 6-in. (15-cm) Ordnance Survey sheets for Yorkshire showed a number of suspiciously isolated or ruined churches as well as civil parishes (townships) without villages.

4 *The first oblique air photograph of Wharram Percy from the south-east, taken by J. K. S. St Joseph on 22 July 1948. The earthworks are recognizable, but at this early date the art of taking good shadow photographs had not been perfected. At the top centre is the crop-mark of a Romano-British enclosure which was not noticed at the time.*

A glorious June, 1948

In June 1948 the study of deserted villages took a number of considerable leaps forward. Some of the first air photographs specifically of village sites were taken for the Cambridge University Collection (4), and international recognition of the subject was ensured by a seminar in Cambridge attended by Axel Steensberg, pioneer excavator of villages in Denmark.

What is more, Beresford was able on that occasion to report to the seminar that what had previously seemed a Midland phenomenon now had no frontier, and that a methodical parish-by-parish examination of the Vale of York and the Yorkshire Wolds had commenced. A first step was an examination of the Ordnance Survey map for parish names that were not matched any longer by villages, and thus the name Wharram Percy, a parish with a suspiciously isolated church, was first encountered. A visit to it was planned for the weekend after the Cambridge seminar. Two school friends, Eric and Philip Lawton, then ex-Service students, were free from their examinations and able to join Beresford for a walking weekend. Beresford was anxious to see a village site in the Yorkshire Wolds, an area that he had never visited, and a booking was made at Malton Youth Hostel, which was within reach of Wharram Percy.

On the morning of Saturday 26 June, hostel duties done, they caught a local bus to Birdsall from which an attractive web of footpaths climbed the Wolds towards Wharram. In the event most of these proved to be victims of wartime and post-war ploughing, so the three explorers eventually made a circuitous approach to the place where the map showed St Martin's church. After several miles waist-high in corn it was a relief to find a grass field. Most immediately impressive was the almost disused church with the overgrown, tumbling gravestones on the south side of the churchyard (9, 10) and then, on the hill above the church, an astonishing array of earthworks.

Why did the appearance of these earthworks astonish when so many had already been encountered during fieldwork in the Midlands? The answer rested on basic differences in geology. The most familiar Midland sites visited in 1945–8 had been those in Leicestershire, Warwickshire and Northamptonshire, accessible from Rugby on foot or by public transport centred on Rugby, or, from 1947, identifiable in

5 *1955 oblique Cambridge air photograph of a typical Midland clay site – Wolfhampcote, Warwickshire – where the rectangular tofts are visible but no remains of peasant houses. The large enclosure was the moated manor house with the isolated church next to it. Between them, and above the road to the left, may be seen the long dark mark from the unproductive 1954 excavation* (Crown copyright: MOD photograph).

the vertical aerial photographs that had been taken by the Royal Air Force (RAF) and then made available to researchers in the stores at Medmenham. These sites lay where the soils were generally clay and where stone suitable for building did not occur near the surface. At the time when these villages were deserted the manufacture of bricks had not cheapened sufficiently for them to be used in ordinary village houses, whose construction remained basically wood, wattle and daub. In decay these materials lost their form and were easily trampled into the earth by animals. Thus rectangular shapes that might be the remains of houses were rarely seen.

It had not been house remains but another type of earthwork that had enabled the Midland villages to be identified: the centuries-long passage of men, beasts and carts had worn down the unpaved surfaces of the streets until each was a 'hollow way', 3 ft (1 m) or more below the less trodden levels at the house frontages. In wet weather the rain turned the surfaces to mud and accelerated the erosion, particularly where water flowed down a slope. As a result each house now stands virtually on its own, and a village plan can be reconstructed by plotting these platforms. As for the remains of individual houses, the best that can be expected is a rather shapeless patch of lower ground, within a platform, that represents the floor level of the long-decayed building.

The ground occupied by village houses and outbuildings ('tofts') usually had a rectilinear area of private ground ('crofts' or 'garths') at the rear, and boundaries between properties were marked by hedge-banks and ditches rather than by stone walls. The rear of these crofts was often served by a minor access way parallel

6 *1946 Royal Air Force vertical air photograph showing the earthworks very clearly under shadow conditions on a late November afternoon. To the bottom left the surviving ridge and furrow is clearly visible* (Crown copyright: MOD photograph). *North is to the right.*

to the village street, and it too would have its surface lowered by wear. After depopulation the network of house platforms and associated ditches remained. Even after being silted and grassed over, such networks are visible in grass and, where accentuated by low shadows, they are a striking feature of air photographs (**5**).

In the Midland clays the areas of a former village can often be located within the parish by the contrast between its earthworks, as just described, and those of the arable fields beyond the village perimeter. Indeed, the actual perimeter of the crofts often had its prominent bank and ditch to restrain the domestic animals from access to the crops in the fields. Through this bank passed the tracks radiating into the fields, again often preserved as hollow ways. The earthworks created by generations of activity within the arable common fields have a shape and a regularity quite unlike those of houses, crofts and streets. Where the peasant properties in the fields were scattered into arable strips (or 'selions', p. 96) the claylands

usually preserve the selions in ridge and furrow fields, clearest where arable has been long converted to pasture but elsewhere often surviving the levelling action of modern ploughing to show as soil- or crop-marks.

In contrast, the deserted villages of the limestone and chalk regions of England, with their lighter soils, are less likely to have prominent ridge and furrow surviving from their fields – although a block is intact in a paddock west of the present Wharram Percy farm – but where stone was employed as foundations for houses it is more likely to have left in the grass rectilinear earthworks that are recognizably buildings. The same stone foundations have often acted as a deterrent to subsequent ploughing, whether in the eighteenth-century agriculture of Improvement or with the temptations of subsidies in siege economies of the present century. The Wolds are now almost totally under the plough, but almost every one of the many deserted village sites in the neighbourhood of Wharram Percy still has its earthworks on an island of grassland in a sea of arable (for example, Swaythorpe, Pockthorpe, Cottam, Croom, Thirkleby and Towthorpe).

So it was that in June 1948 the footpaths through the high ripening corn gave way to the

7 *1948 Royal Air Force vertical air photograph showing the earthworks in April under dry conditions when the grass over the stone walls is parched, showing them up as white lines* (Crown copyright: MOD photograph).

smoother passage over pasture as the church tower came into sight; and that soon the boundary bank of the village was crossed and the smoothness of the pasture was interrupted by earthworks that needed little skill to be recognized as former croft boundaries and houses. Dimensions of one or two houses were roughly paced out and noted, but there was neither time nor skill for a proper survey. On a subsequent visit to Medmanham it was cheering to find that conditions of light and shadow had been ideal when the RAF cover for this area was taken, and the air photographs (**6**, **7**) aided the interpretation of the earthworks when the first large-scale ground survey came to be made.

A view of the site

A visitor to the site will still see the village earthworks very much as they were in 1948, for English Heritage's programme of display and interpretation for visitors has marked out the position of the earthworks removed by the large-scale excavations at Areas 6 and 10 between 1953 and 1970. The earlier superficial excavations at Areas 5, 12, 15, 17, 18 and 20 in 1950–2 (p. 27) did not remove house walls, and all the trenches then excavated were infilled and have become grass covered again.

The first earthworks of which most visitors become aware will be those hollow ways that have resulted from the passage of traffic in the past. The footpath approach from the public car park near Bella Farm follows one such deeply-worn track that formerly connected the village to Towthorpe with its parish church at Wharram Percy and was the only means of access to Wharram for wheeled vehicles until 1962. At the lower end of this path the large-scale movement of earth for the making of the Burdale railway tunnel has obscured the original track, but after crossing the former railway cutting its line, although widened for modern use, is followed by the present road leading towards the church. Hollow ways of original dimensions will be seen approaching this road from the right (west), and any of these will take the visitor up to the plateau where the main line of village houses stood (Buildings 4 to 17) and where the house earthworks are the most distinct. As Figure **2** shows, the visitor

8 (right) *The North Manor. Above: a conjectural reconstruction of the manor in the thirteenth century. Below: an interpretation plan of the earthworks.*

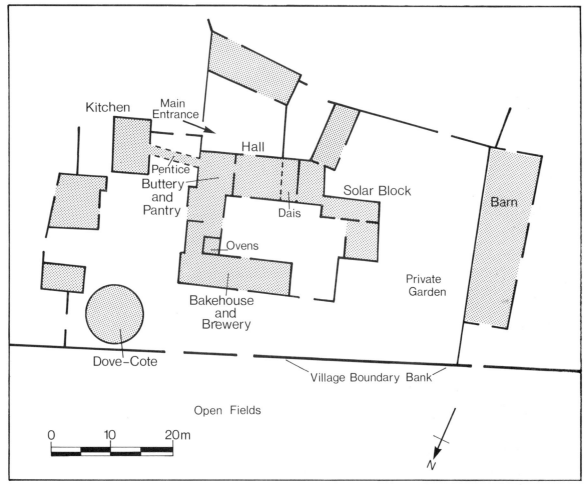

Kitchen

Main Entrance

Hall

Pentice

Buttery and Pantry

Dais

Solar Block

Ovens

Bakehouse and Brewery

Private Garden

Barn

Dove–Cote

Village Boundary Bank

Open Fields

0   10   20m

N

will have already passed the earthworks of three houses on the left (east) of the approach road, but these are not of the best quality and will have more meaning after the other Buildings are experienced. In the course of the climb the visitor will appreciate how the choice of site necessitated a strenuous carriage of water from the springs and the stream in the valley floor; no wells have been discovered in the course of excavations.

On the hillside the village tracks now appear as sloping terraces in the grass. On the plateau they deepen again into hollow ways, the most prominent being that which led north-westwards towards New Malton, the principal regional market place after a borough was founded there in the early twelfth century. On the right (north) of this track the complex of small earthworks was sufficiently different from those of the peasant long-houses for it to be dubbed in 1948, even without excavation, 'the manor house area' and its components designated as dining hall, kitchen, dovecote and barn (8).

Elsewhere the pattern of earthworks is dominated by the long line of village houses, mostly lying east-west with their western ends merging into the gentle slope of the plateau. On the other three sides sufficient wall footings remain for upstanding grass banks, although low, to be recognized as house walls marking out the characteristic shape of the 'long-house' (see 2); several have a gap in one of their longer sides, the remains of a doorway. Internal divisions between human and animal occupation are too flimsy to appear on the surface, so that within the walls the grass is usually level. However the organic and burned matter accumulating on the floor around the hearth encourages the growth of nettles and thus identifies the humans' end of the house.

With experience, and aided by the interpretative markers now provided by English Heritage, the earthworks around the individual long-houses begin to acquire meaning: a spacious farmyard, sometimes with small outbuildings; a wall on the street side, broken by an entrance; and in every case a dividing bank between the territory of one house and its neighbour.

The only upstanding medieval building is the parish church of St Martin (9, 10). Its fabric and that of earlier churches revealed by excavation are described at pp. 52–63. The last of what had become an annual Ramblers' (or Harvest)

9 *General view of the parish church of St Martin in 1954 from the south-west before the collapse of the tower. The crack may be seen running up the tower, and the slates are beginning to slip off the roof. The blocked-up arcades of the south aisle may be seen.*

10 *General view of St Martin in 1956 from the north-west taken before the collapse of the tower. Only a few slates are missing from the roof. The blocked up arcade of the north aisle may be seen.*

Service was held in July 1949, but after a service in August 1949, attended by the patron of the living, Lord Middleton, there was to be no other for 33 years (p. 53). Although the church still had its font, pews, lectern, altar and bells, disrepair was everywhere visible: the tower was badly cracked, slates were missing and the plaster ceiling was decayed by rain and nesting pigeons. In the graveyard many tombstones were cracked and leaning.

Animals were barred from the graveyard by post and rail fencing, also in need of repair, and on the south side a farm gate gave access to what had once been the track across the Wolds to Thixendale, a village whose inhabitants had been parishioners of St Martin's until their landlord, Sir Tatton Sykes, provided them with their own church in 1870. The track, across rough country, was thereafter little used, and a further deterrent was the waterlogged valley bottom next to the churchyard with a disused sheep wash and the silted up remains of the medieval mill pond.

In the valley by the church there were no earthworks to indicate where the excavations would later uncover a series of vicarage buildings. The line of three nineteenth-century agricultural labourers' cottages nearby were

still occupied in 1948 and their gardens cultivated (4), but the gardeners could have had no idea that just beyond a spade's depth were the buried walls of the single farmstead (89) from which the whole township was farmed in the three-and-a-half centuries between the depopulation and the building of Wharram Percy High House, now Wharram Percy Farm (11), sometime between 1846 and 1851.

To appreciate the extent and character of the agricultural land available to the villagers it is necessary to return to the plateau from the valley by one of the many terraced tracks. The open situation on the plateau brings easily into one view the spread of house sites for the full length of the village before the ground dips into Drue Dale. Towards the northern end of the village, near the manor house earthworks, there is in clear weather a fine long-distance view across the Vale of Pickering to the North Yorkshire Moors. In the opposite direction, across the valley and higher than the top of the church tower, the Wolds extend eastward, and here in the right season the growing corn carries broad bands of differential colouring.

11 *The south front of the mid-nineteenth-century Wharram Percy farm with the Midgley family in the foreground. They were the tenant farmers from the 1940s until 1980.*

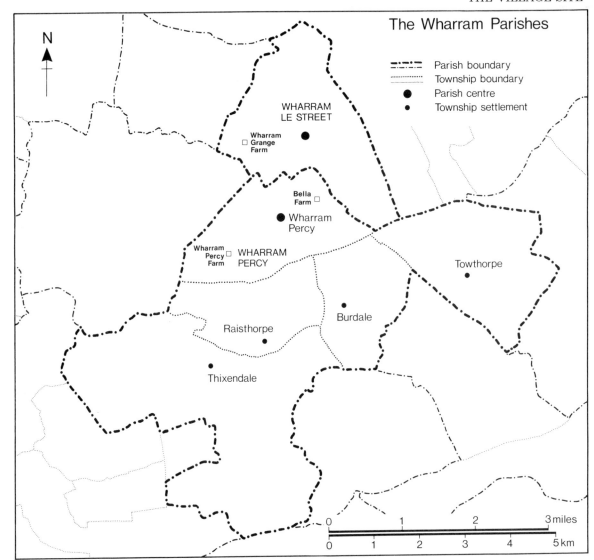

The Wharram Parishes

–·–·–	Parish boundary
··········	Township boundary
●	Parish centre
•	Township settlement

WHARRAM LE STREET ●

Wharram Grange Farm □

Bella Farm □

● Wharram Percy

Wharram Percy Farm □ WHARRAM PERCY

Towthorpe •

Burdale •

Raisthorpe •

Thixendale •

N

0   1   2   3 miles
0   1   2   3   4   5 km

12 *Map showing the two parishes of Wharram le Street and Wharram Percy. Wharram le Street, a single township with only a sub-division at Wharram Grange (as it was also divided in Roman times). Wharram Percy had five townships: Wharram Percy and Burdale, deserted about 1500; Raisthorpe and Towthorpe, deserted towards the end of the seventeenth century; and Thixendale, which still survives. The division of Wharram Percy into two farms with the building of Bella Farm (1775–9) is also shown.*

These bands show the crop still responding to the impact on the soil made over the centuries by the villagers' cultivation of the three great open arable Fields in units made up of unhedged strips ('selions').

On the southern horizon is the long line of trees on the prehistoric ridgeway that later shaped the township boundaries of Wharram Percy, Raisthorpe, Thixendale and Towthorpe (**12**). To the south-west, separated by a mile of cornfields, the modern farm bearing the name Wharram Percy is indicated by the trees that form a strong windbreak around it. To the north near the Visitor's Car Park is a second farm, Bella, built in 1774–6. The whole Wharram Percy township is now (1989) cultivated from these two farms under sheep-and-corn husbandry, with cattle on the permanent grassland in the steep-sided dales (and in parts of the village site). Thus Wharram Percy farm is the most recent in a series of short-distance relocations of the centre of settlement from which the agricultural resources of the township were exploited, although the chronology and causation of these movements were unknowns in 1948.

Return to the site, 1950–2

Although Beresford had acquired considerable experience in the interpretation of the historical landscape of the Midlands, he was quite untrained in the techniques of excavation and had been driven to undertake his archaeology at Stretton Baskerville, Warwicks., only by the hope that simple excavation would confirm that the earthworks had been correctly interpreted as medieval villages. Candidly put, this aspect of his work could be summed up in the words of Hoskin's estimate of his own achievements at Hamilton, Leics., which were taking place at the same time: 'My "excavation" is best forgotten'. In the two years following the first visit to Wharram his main energy was devoted to combing documents for historical evidence from Yorkshire sites detected on maps, on air photographs or in the field.

Excavations were a relaxation, conducted on a one-day basis at weekends if student volunteers were forthcoming and only on sites accessible from Leeds by public transport (Wilstrop, Yorks., W. R., and East Lilling, Yorks., N. R.). The editor of the *Yorkshire Archaeological*

13 *The estate gamekeeper, Mr Stillwell, and Mr and Mrs Milner outside the west cottage garden at Wharram Percy about 1950.*

Journal agreed to find space for a historical gazetteer of deserted sites in all three Ridings (published in 1951–4), and thus the basic documentary evidence for Wharram Percy came to be collected alongside that for other villages in the Wolds without any intention of returning to excavate there. The fine RAF vertical photograph of the village site took its place in the files alongside many others from Yorkshire.

Yet in June 1950 Miss Myrtle Milner, living with her parents, brother and sister at the Wharram Percy labourers' cottage (13) made the following entries in her diary:

> Friday June 9th. The students arrived to do some excavating … Sunday 11th. The students have found some pieces of pot, a bone needle and part of a knife or dagger and they haven't dug very deep. They are coming next weekend too.

The return to Wharram had been strangely brought about: on 10 October 1949 Beresford had given a broadcast talk for BBC North Region, to celebrate the 600th anniversary of the Black Death, in which he argued that the plague of 1349, serious as it was, had permanently destroyed very few English villages even though local lore often attributed deserted villages to it. He instanced the now-flourishing village of Settrington where heavy plague mortality was documented, and if time had permitted he could have added the evidence from Wharram Percy itself where the evidence from documents was clear: although the lord of the manor, Walter de Heslerton, had died of the plague in September 1349 (and perhaps the vicar also in the same month), a survey of the manor made in 1368 accounted for some 30 occupied houses, and 30 taxpayers were recorded at the poll tax collection of 1377, while manorial surveys of 1435 and 1458 agreed that there were still at least 16 houses.

That broadcast happened to be heard by Mr Winstanley, headmaster of the village school at Settrington, which had Wharram le Street and Wharram Percy within its catchment area. He wrote to say that he had heard that next to Wharram Percy church there was the site of a village destroyed by the plague – inadvertently illustrating the unhistorical lore – and added that, should there ever be any possibility of organizing an excavation, he was sure that the site owner, then the 11th Baron Middleton of Birdsall House, whom he knew as chairman of

14 *North Manor excavations 1950 with the first excavation team (left to right) Peter Tillott, Keith Allison, June Milner, Ted Milner, Maurice Beresford, Mr Winstanley and Terry Milner.*

his school managers, would be interested and give permission; and he went on to offer the use of his schoolroom for overnight accommodation.

It was a remarkably fortuitous offer, for he had no idea that Beresford already knew the site and had been impressed by its earthworks,

15 *Building 15: the first excavation of a peasant house at Wharram in 1950. At this stage, before any archaeological input to the site, Beresford was simply searching for walls.*

nor that excavations at the two Yorkshire clayland sites had proved disappointing, making an exploration on the chalk all the more attractive. The offer was gladly accepted, and arrangements were made to recruit a small weekend party in the period after university examinations. Its equipment was as primitive as its archaeological technique. Mr Winstanley himself joined in, and the two younger Milner children were pressed into service (**14**). The visitors slept on trestle tables or bare boards in the schoolroom, ensuring that they were awake early enough to make the journey to Wharram station where the car was parked before the final journey up the valley to the site.

The intention and the technique employed were no more advanced than at Beresford's earlier excavations: to find house wall foundations – which had eluded him in the clayland sites in the Midlands and the Vale of York – and datable materials that would show whether the buildings did have a life up to, but not beyond, the beginning of the sixteenth century. A start was made at the earthworks (Buildings 15; see **2** and **15**) that most resembled a house, having an apparent entrance in the long south side. Wall foundations of up to three courses of roughly-faced stone appeared as soon as the turf was removed, and, as Miss Milner's diary entry shows, the top soil contained artefacts. The field was being grazed at that time, and the agreement with the farmer was that no trenches should be left open. Miss Milner's diary for the Saturday of the subsequent weekend shows that work had been resumed and that again the site was proving productive, even including a skeleton that had been buried mysteriously under the threshold of House 15:

> On arriving at Wharram at night I was informed that a skeleton had been found and on Sunday there was heaps of people over to see the skeleton, [christened] 'Percy'. Mr Beresford and party left about 5 or 6 pm. They had all enjoyed themselves. The kids [her younger brother and sister, Terry and June] had a good time too. Helping to wash up and dig for pot etc.

That weekend also saw the first exploration of the earthworks at the north end of the village (Building D, **2**), which seemed different from houses. Sections were dug where Buildings 17 and 18 touched the banks of the hollow way

16 *The manorial demesne at Wharram Percy, 1436, from the Inquisition after the death of William Hilton, 28 July 1435. Line 7:* est quidam scitus man[er]ii qui nichil val[et] per annu[m] *(there is the site of the manor, worth nothing). Line 9:* sunt ib[ide]m xvi mesuagia *(there are 16 messuages [houses]). Line 11:* est ib[ide]m unu[m] molendin[ium] aquaticum ad blada *(there is a water mill for corn).*

and at several points in the complex where much more substantial walls gave credence to the idea of a manor house. It was assumed that the lord of the manor had lived in this area as long as there had been a village (but see p. 47 below) and that the walls would certainly relate to the manor house that had been mentioned in surveys of 1323, 1367 and 1368 that followed the deaths of members of the Percy family and also in 1436 and 1458 following the deaths of two members of the Hilton family (**16**) after the Percies had exchanged the manor at the beginning of that century for one nearer their principal estates at Warkworth and Alnwick in Northumberland.

The pottery was submitted to the Yorkshire Museum where it was accepted as medieval.

Encouraged by these forays and by offers of help in surveying from an architectural historian at the University of Manchester, two further weekends of work were arranged for 8 and 15 June 1951. 'Mr Beresford and the students came again,' recorded Miss Milner, 'They are sleeping in the [Wharram le Street] school this time.'

After establishing the four corners of the walling of Building 12 and the position of its doorway, it was decided to follow round the complete circuit of walls at another site (see **2**, **20**) which lay separately from the main line of long houses. Portions of level earth floorings were also exposed, but no search was taken deeper. In the four weekends of 1950 and 1951 one of the initial objectives had been met: these were certainly medieval village houses.

By the time that excavations were arranged for 20 and 27 June 1952 it was known that two young Cambridge graduates in archaeology had become interested in the subject. One of them had gone to dig in Denmark with Steensberg by the time that digging began. When the other, John Hurst, arrived, he found work in progress at Building 5, chosen because the alignment of the longer side of the earth-

29

17 *Area 5: the excavation of the south-east corner by Beresford in June 1952 first demonstrating a sequence of building periods.*

works was north-south, in contrast with the east-west alignment elsewhere. The southern wall of the house was exposed by trenching to the depth of its foundations, and a transverse section was dug across the floor. Although their significance as the remains of earlier buildings was not realized, this section encountered the foundations of other walls protruding at a level lower than the floor. It had been naively assumed until then that the houses that gave rise to the earthworks (here and elsewhere) had always occupied the same site (**17**).

Hurst at once recognized the evidence for an occupational sequence. He had had an archaeological training and possessed an awareness of new techniques of excavating and recording that would be appropriate for following sequences of building on the same site. From the historian's point of view, at a time when changes in the standard of living over the medieval centuries were being much discussed the possibility of sequential archaeological evidence raised quite new possibilities. 'You will be coming to professionalise our amateur questionings', wrote Beresford to Hurst.

After the second weekend it was possible to make plans confidently for a larger-scale excavation in 1953. There was now a hope that more might now come from Wharram Percy than the confirmation of an early-sixteenth-century depopulation date, and Hurst's offer to take over the archaeological directorship was accepted, even though his ideas of founding an organized Research Group that August seemed rather alien to the individualistic traditions of a desk historian.

2

Early excavations

Plans and expectations, 1952–3

When Hurst first communicated with Beresford on 23 January 1952 he was a postgraduate research student at Cambridge having obtained a degree in archaeology. Like students of archaeology elsewhere, medieval archaeology had formed no part of his course. Academic interest in the material remains of that period was confined to castles, monasteries, parish churches and manor houses, and this interest was predominantly that of architectural historians. Few of the lesser medieval buildings survived to illustrate the character of ordinary village houses: most house sites were still occupied by houses of a later period, preventing excavation, and only sporadic excavation had taken place on sites where habitation had been permanently abandoned.

Here and there, sites with whole villages abandoned had been noticed by local antiquaries and historians, beginning with John Rous in Warwickshire in 1492. County historians such as Dugdale (1656) and Bridges (1719) had identified the earthworks of such sites in their published works, but excavation had not followed. Even when an intellectual interest in excavation became widespread among antiquarians from the 1840s onwards it was rarely aroused by village sites, preferring remains from further antiquity.

In the years immediately before 1939 small excavations at Seacourt, Berks., and Great Beere, Devon, showed the potential of archaeology at deserted village sites, but after the interruption of the Second World War these had not been followed up. Hurst's awareness of deserted medieval villages came from conversations with a fellow-student of archaeology, Jack Golson, early in 1951. Golson had previously been a student of history, had heard of depopulated settlements from lectures by Professor Postan and was now hopeful that archaeology might throw light on some of the questions where documents did not seem to assist, particularly the structure of the peasant house. Excavation of a medieval site also seemed likely to provide material for Hurst's researches into pottery, and the two resolved to collaborate. Thus Hurst came to Wharram Percy to observe Beresford's work in progress while Golson went to Denmark where advanced techniques of open area excavation (p. 33 below) were being practised.

Hurst was immediately impressed by what he saw at Wharram and during the summer worked to prepare a lecture for the British Association

18 *Hurst and Beresford in 1975 looking at the fourteenth-century stone wall bounding the north side of the churchyard.*

meeting, drawing attention to the archaeological potential of deserted village sites. He became convinced that several academic disciplines would have to be involved and by November had organized the launch of a Deserted Medieval Village Research Group. In December it was agreed that Wharram Percy was the best available site for a research excavation.

At that time the archaeological aims were limited and selective. There was no thought that the project might last 40 years nor that a church and a manor house would be investigated: nothing more was envisaged than the complete investigation of a single peasant house, such as those' that Beresford's trial excavations had demonstrated might be expected under each of the rectangular earthworks in the field. The earthwork at Area 10 was selected simply because it lay nearest to the proposed excavation base in the surviving labourers' cottages.

The main problems in the early years were difficulties of access by a track that ran through cornfields and a certain restiveness on the part

19 *Area 10: general view from the west in 1953, showing a rectangular earthwork, of the latest building with the turf and topsoil removed to reveal the general rubble level A2. The two baulks are still in place. In the background the trees in Nut Wood had just been planted.*

of the tenant farmer, despite Lord Middleton's continual support. A lack of funds was an impediment for the first 20 years, during which the work was carried out almost all by volunteers with only small equipment grants from various bodies. With such limited resources the project could never have developed had not Professor H. C. Darby recruited and financed an annual field party of students from the Department of Geography, University College, London. They formed the main core of volunteers during the 1950s and 1960s and enabled the period of work to be extended from the weekends of 1950–2 to an annual three-week season. No more could be envisaged while the supervisors and organizer were giving up their holidays to direct the projects and a charge was being levied on all volunteers for their food.

Progress was also limited by the unexpected complexity of the site and the labour-intensive method of excavation. Thus in the first season the work advanced no further than the stripping of turf and subsoil from the rectangular earthwork; it would have been too ambitious at that time to have thought of opening up the whole area of the toft. It was realized from work on the Continent, especially Denmark, that medieval peasant houses were flimsy, had insubstantial foundations and might well have been frequently rebuilt on different alignments. Thus the accepted method of Roman and prehis-

20 *Area 10: general view from the west showing the stage A3 with the general rubble removed to expose the various wall alignments.*

toric archaeology – dividing up a site into a regimented pattern of regular trenches on a grid plan – would be unsuitable.

An open-area excavation was therefore planned, following the experience gained by Golson in his six-months' work in Denmark. It was the first time that open-area excavation had been seen at a medieval site in England, it having been demonstrated previously only by the German archaeologist, Bersu, in the 1930s at the Iron Age farm of Little Woodbury, Wilts., and on a Viking site in the Isle of Man in the 1940s. Open-area excavation is now an archaeological norm but in 1953 it was very daring. In the same way that Beresford's peers discounted claims of settlement depopulation, so the archaeological establishment thought it most unwise for an area to be opened up without leaving 'Baulks' – narrow unexcavated strips between the trenches where there would be a preserved record of all the layers encountered as the excavation deepened.

In fact, being only two years from graduation, and cautious, Golson and Hurst did leave two baulks across the area opened over the earth-work of Building 10. This made barrowing easier but proved to be disastrous since the layers that they recorded in section showed very little, certainly failing to elucidate the sequence, and crucial changes were concealed until the baulks were removed. This seems to be a problem very often: a baulk proves to be positioned over the very place where the archaeological levels are such that the sequence is quite different on either side of the baulk. Even though the baulks were carefully removed at the final stage of Area 10 it was still not possible to answer some of the vital questions that had arisen, such as where features of different periods met (**20**).

The methods employed have been fully described elsewhere. Basically they consisted of taking off the turf, then cleaning up the exposed surface (which was designated *A1*). This surface was planned, and spot heights levelled at 2ft 6-in. (0.76-m) intervals, following a similar survey at turf level before excavation. In a second stage (*A2*) all small stones not obviously parts of walls were removed, leaving in place all large stones and all others that might eventually be parts of walls *in situ* or have fallen when the walls collapsed or were demolished. All the stones were plotted and levelled with the idea of making as complete a record as possible (**22**), since at this stage in Area 10 very few actual wall lines were appar-

22 *Area 10: the recording of finds in a 5-ft (1.3-
m) square by the project surveyor, R. T. Porter,
in 1957.*

ent (**colour plate 12**). The third, and most
difficult, stage (*A3*) was to remove all stones
that semed to have fallen from the wall or be
random with the expectation of exposing the
walls themselves (**20**). The excavation then
progressed in the same way, recording walls
that were encountered on different alignments
with *B* numbers and the natural chalk underneath (with signs of timber buildings cut into
it) as *C*.

Peasant houses
In the event the results were much more complex than had been envisaged for it very soon
became clear that the buildings in Area 10 were
not confined to the rectangle of ground that had
been opened up under the surface earthwork.

---

21 (left)   *Area 10: view from the south of a line
of superimposed chalk walls at the east end of
the excavation.*

Fragments of walls were found extending in
all directions beyond the area opened up. In
subsequent years the open area was extended
until eventually all the eastern portion of the
toft was excavated. This did provide evidence
for the main medieval structures, but with
hindsight the whole toft should have been
uncovered layer by layer, for more recent work
has shown that there were medieval outbuildings to the west of the main structure with
extensive Saxon occupation underneath them.

Thus although the results obtained in the
1950s were in a sense misleading, it was felt
necessary at the time to progress by moving to
a second house site elsewhere in the village to
see how typical the houses in Area 10 would
be, the more so in view of the additional
complexities raised by the discovery of a manor
house under part of Area 10 (below, p. 44). With
the limited resources of the time the decision
could be justified, but it does demonstrate the
lesson, seen time and time again at Wharram,
that even quite large-scale excavation can produce only partial results (p. 76).

In the 1960s, with resources still limited,

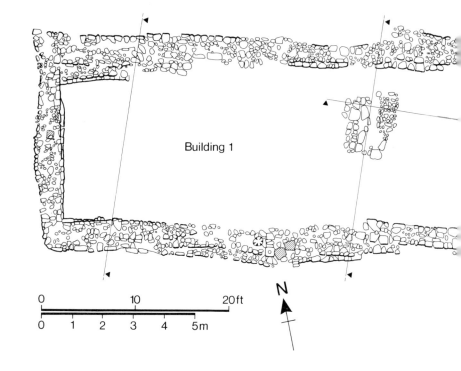

Building 1

0   10   20ft

0 1 2 3 4 5m

N

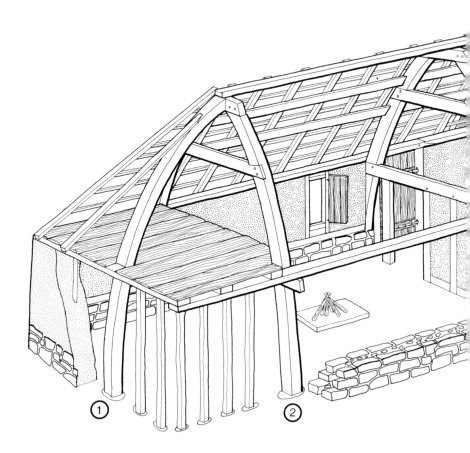

① ②

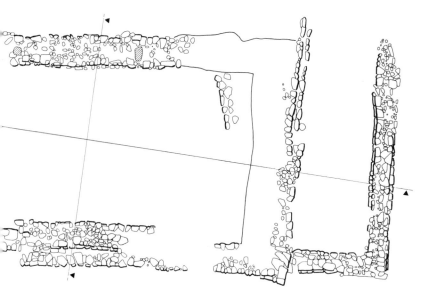

23 *Area 6. Above: plan of the latest fifteenth-century long-house with its short stretches of wall on different alignments typical of a cruck-built house. Below: a reconstruction of the super-structure of a cruck building showing three different methods of seating crucks. 1 and 2 are earthfast in a post-hole; 3 and 4 are on a ground-wall.*

the priority still lay with the question of the peasant house. It is surprising that Beresford's excavations before 1953 had found solid chalk walls in each of the earthworks and yet in Area 10 only small lengths of wall could be found on the various alignments (21). It was hoped that Area 6, which lay on the plateau immediately above the church and adjoining earthworks that had yielded walls to three courses in 1952, might furnish more substantial structures. With a length of nearly 100 ft (30 m), its earthwork was twice as long as in Area 10.

The method of excavation at Area 6 (**colour plate 11**) followed that of Area 10 but the results were more easily interpreted: chalk foundations of a substantial long-house with a stone hearth, opposing doorways and a lower unheated east part (23). Walls were not straight, and at the time these were interpreted as following from constant rebuilding of the peasant house, as at Area 10. Other chalk founda-

24 *Area 6: general view from the west of the latest fifteenth-century long-house, with the short lengths of chalk foundations on different alignments plainly in view. These are now interpreted as non load-bearing walls between the crucks.*

tions were found that were then interpreted as earlier buildings, and – most importantly – postholes and slots survived from timber buildings earlier than any made from chalk. This confirmed the fact that, even in areas where building stone was available locally, it was not used to build peasant houses until the thirteenth century at the earliest, the Saxon tradition of timber buildings continuing right through the early medieval period.

In the 1950s and 1960s the complex sequence of buildings in Areas 10 and 6 was interpreted as a series of peasant houses constantly rebuilt on different alignments since at the time it was expected that the peasant house would be flimsy and short-lived, basically because there seemed to be no survivals but also because of continental evidence. When the excavations of the two Areas were eventually published these views were modified, and it was suggested that rebuilding took place at longer intervals. More recently the position has been reviewed, especially taking into account evidence from vernacular buildings that was not available 30 years ago. This revision shows how interpretation of evidence depended on the archaeologists' expectations at the time.

Although it was known that cruck building was a feature of the North Yorkshire Moors and the Vale of Pickering it was not thought to extend further south into the Wolds. In fact there was already published evidence for crucks surviving in the Wolds into the nineteenth century, and it would now seem to have been the typical construction at Wharram. Walls built by the cruck method do not support the roof and are therefore flimsy, simply acting as an outside skin, as in a modern steel-framed building (23). Thus the flimsiness of the walls that were found did not necessarily denote slight buildings. Since they were built in short stretches between cruck and cruck they did not have to be in a continuous line and could be repaired every few years without replacing the roof. The latest building in Area 6 could have had a life of a century or more, however frequently its flimsy walls were repaired or replaced. Evidence has now been found of

25 *Cambridge vertical air photograph of the deserted medieval village of Thorálby, to the east of Duggleby, 1 mile (1.6 km) to the east of Wharram le Street along the Gypsey Race. This village was not deserted until the seventeenth century, for, besides the medieval long-houses, earthworks are visible of courtyard farms that developed only in the sixteenth century.*

several padstones, and thus many of the buildings can now be divided into bays. Indeed, the presence of pivot stones for hanging doors and of hinges among the material finds should already have shown that doors were solid framed rather than wattle, or mat or sacking hangings. Smaller hinges could have come from framed windows with shutters, and the keys found suggest not only private property to be secured but also walls that were too solid to be broken through.

As the shape of the surface earthworks suggested, the main plan form was the long-house, comprising a building under one roof and divided into three parts: an inner room for sleeping or for a dairy; a main living room with a central hearth on its floor; and after a cross passage a third room for a cattle byre or other farming uses at the lower end (26). Over the last 40 years excavations have shown that this house-type was much more widespread over Britain than the restricted distribution of surviving examples above ground had suggested.

Exactly how the long-house fits in to the development of house types is still debatable. Evidence from both Area 10 and Area 6 suggested that the fourteenth- and fifteenth-century long-houses were preceded by shorter and smaller houses without a byre or a lower farm part, although Wrathmell has recently

26 *A general reconstruction of daily life in a typical medieval cruck-built long-house, with the cattle at the lower end in the foreground, a cross-passage and the domestic part of the house behind with a central hearth.*

proposed that these were remains of once longer houses. He has also suggested that within each toft there was not just a single long-house with no outbuildings but also small barns, previously interpreted as earlier houses. Later work at the rear of the long-houses in Tofts 10 and 17 has also revealed foundations of substantial outbuildings.

It is not known what lay in the rest of Toft 6, since it was not completely excavated. It is also possible that Toft 10, originally separate from Toft 9, was amalgamated with it in the fifteenth century, making the earthwork in 9 a living house and that in 10 a barn. This would resolve oddities in the structure of the latest building in 10 and the lack of firm evidence for a hearth. Most medieval peasant tofts in the area appear to have single long-house earthworks. It is not till the sixteenth century that courtyard farms became common (25).

These problems demonstrate how necessary it is to excavate a complete toft before drawing firm conclusions. Present techniques do not allow finds to be dated to a band narrower than 25, and some would say 50, years. It is therefore difficult to determine which buildings in different parts of the same croft were contemporary. It is also not as easy as it might seem to determine the use of particular buildings. One might expect material finds from the living quarters of a house to be different from those in the others, but an analysis of finds from the two buildings (possibly contemporary) within Area 6 was not conclusive in showing that the more southerly building was a long-house and the other a barn.

There remain other uncertainties: were there always small houses before long-houses? Was development in Tofts 6 and 10 determined by special features? Indeed, was there such a thing as a typical toft? Only the excavation of all the tofts would answer that question. Perhaps it was naive in 1952 to expect that sequences of development could be determined from the excavation of anything less.

Daily life

Likewise with the evidence for medieval peasant life: a lot has been found out but many problems still remain. In Areas 10 and 6 in the 1950s and 1960s, different types of object were plotted on to plans in different colours (**colour plate 12**) and the depth and position of all significant finds recorded in detail. It was

hoped, with the expected constant rebuilding, to identify the different floor levels and to date the finds from the various periods by the pottery. Again, like the houses themselves, the archaeological deposits they contained were much more complex. Although the records show the levels of the important objects, and the layers from which they came are described, it is not easy to link these with the sequence of structures.

No distinct occupation levels were found, unlike Steensberg's excavations in Denmark. This was partly due to the fact, important in itself, that medieval peasants do not seem to have been as messy and uncivilized as had been suspected: they did not leave accumulated rubbish deposits of the type often found on Roman sites, which were supposedly more civilized. The houses also seem to have been cleaned so thoroughly that not only are there few finds associated with each structure but the sweeping was so frequent that hollows developed that have themselves caused problems with the stratigraphy and with the stability of the structures.

The difficulty of closely dating the pottery is made worse in Yorkshire since the most common domestic pottery used at Wharram, made at kilns 14 miles (20 km) away in the Vale of Pickering at Staxton and Potter Brompton, had a long date range of some 200 years during which the same fabric derived from the same clays. This pottery was continually used, so it is hard to give precise dating to most pottery fragments. Likewise the presence of household or farming objects has not led to firm conclusions about the interpretation of buildings. Some may have been built for one purpose and then re-used for another. Then when they have been demolished, and turned into a yard churned up by animals, it is almost impossible to tell which finds came from the first use of a building, which from its re-use or which post-dated its destruction. Here we are once more up against the limitations of the archaeological evidence, which are more acute on a rural domestic site than at a castle or monastery, which is likely to have more clearly defined areas of activity lasting over longer periods. One only has to look at modern farms where a new house has been built, and the old farmhouse converted to farm use, to see some of the problems.

The major question of rubbish disposal, how-

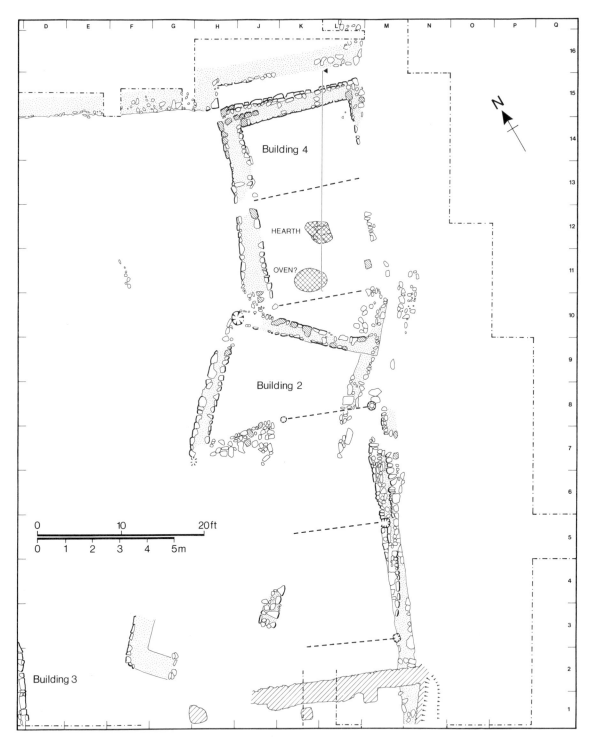

27 *Area 10: plan of fourteenth- and fifteenth-century peasant buildings on different alignments.*

28 *Outside activities in the fields.*

ever, has important implications for the archaeological evidence. Only two rubbish pits from the medieval period have been found at Wharram. The yards were remarkably clean, and in particular the large quarries, from which the building stone was extracted in each toft, were backfilled with clean rubble with only the odd pottery fragment being found (31).

The main rubbish seems to have been collected into middens and then put on the fields as manure. That found in the tofts was only the residue that had not been spread on the boundary banks. This is confirmed by the large amounts of pottery found on the open fields that have been manured with household rubbish. Yet this seems to have applied only in the medieval and Roman periods, for there is much Saxon rubbish dumped in the tofts. The lack of Saxon pottery on the fields may therefore not be because it was friable and has not survived but because manure was not spread on the fields at this period. This practice seems common on many Saxon rural sites, where large quantities of rubbish have been found in the settlement itself.

The various objects found in the peasant tofts do, however, give interesting glimpses of medieval peasant life. Small hinges from chests and caskets, together with keys, again show the sense of private property and the possibility of burglary and theft. This may also suggest that the whole family would go out into the fields together, for if the wife and children were left at home there would surely not be so much need for security.

The fragments of pottery, iron, copper alloy and bone give important evidence for the various activities that took place in the home, some of which are depicted in Figure 26. As most of the furniture would have been of wood there is little evidence for it except the metal fittings already mentioned. Items of dress fittings tell us about clothes and how they were worn. The pottery comprised mainly cooking pots and bowls for food preparation and serving, including large bowls for dairy products. Jugs are rare, but this may not mean that liquid containers were not used but rather that they were made of leather or wood. Similarly, basket work does not normally survive.

Pottery firecovers for retaining the fire at night were found, but the more elaborate pottery items like chafing dishes for keeping food warm and money boxes were rare or absent,

showing the basic simplicity of the forms used. But in stark contrast there were, in both peasant Houses 10 and 6, fragments of exotic pottery jugs, not only from the south-west of France but also tin-glazed maiolica from the Mediterranean. Neither is to be expected in a peasant house, but it is uncertain whether these single examples show higher status or were cast offs from the manor house. Some of the metal objects were also of high quality.

Other activities in the home besides food preparation are shown: spindle whorls were used for spinning; needles, thimbles and scissors are evidence for sewing, and candle holders suggest that the medieval peasant did not always retire to bed at dark. Recreation is shown by bone flutes, dice and Nine Men's Morris (**colour plate 6**). Other activities in the village generally are suggested in the reconstructed scenes (28). The wide range of animal bones shows the various types of animals kept and eaten and their various by-products: hides, wool and dairy produce.

Many of the sites produced large quantities of horse bones, some showing marks resulting from the use of horses for traction, so that much of the medieval ploughing on the light chalk soils at Wharram may have been done by horses and not by the traditional oxen of the clay Midlands. This may be one reason for the exceptionally long strips in the open fields. It is also possible that horses were bred in the medieval period at Wharram. There is medieval evidence for this, and horses are still a feature of the Malton area.

A manor house

In only the third season of excavation in 1955 came the first of many major surprises over the 40 years of excavation. In the north-west corner of the excavation in Area 10 a major wall was found: a trench showed that the base of the wall was 10ft (3m) below the turf. This was the first sign of the sunken undercroft of a major late-twelfth-century manor house, completely unexpected since it was assumed that, whatever changes there might be to peasant houses, the main structures of the village – its church, vicarage and manor house – would be static. In fact the positions of all three were found to have altered, but this was the first hint at Wharram of this constant pattern of change. Whatever the discovery of a manor house meant in terms of opening up new possibilities, it was

29 *Area 10 Manor House: the undercroft fully excavated in 1957, with the sandstone threshold in the foreground, then the three supporting pillar bases for the floor above and, behind, the projecting fireplace.*

a blow to the expectation that in Area 10 the peasant houses would stretch back through early medieval to Saxon times.

The excavation of the manor house undercroft, spread over 1956 and 1957 (**colour plate 10**) showed a major building 38 ft 8 in. (11.9 m) × 17 ft 4 in. (5.28 m) set 10 ft (3 m) into the ground at the west end and 6 ft 6 in. (2 m) at the east. It was constructed of roughly coursed chalk blocks with sandstone dressings. Most medieval undercrofts were set at ground level so that the main apartment was at first floor level, but at Wharram the undercroft was a cellar and the main room was at ground floor level. This was very economical, for the quarrying of the chalk to build the walls formed space for the cellar. There was a projecting base for a fireplace and three stone bases for wooden pillars to support the floor above (**29**). Large numbers of carved sandstone pieces that had collapsed into the cellar made it possible to make a reconstruction drawing (**97**).

It has been interpreted as the solar block of a manor house, providing the private accommodation for the lord, to which would be attached a public timber hall. The foundations for the east wall of this survived by the side of the ramp down into the undercroft, but the rest had been destroyed by later activities. In colour plate **9** an attempt has been made to show how the manor may have looked. The building is datable to the last quarter of the twelfth century by the waterleaf capitals and waterholding bases of the supports for the firehood and by the general character of the remains of the door and window surrounds. Subsequently, traces of cesspits, a cold store and a possible haystack base were found at the rear of the enclosure within which the manor house stood (p. 77).

Historical documentation of the settlement that was eventually named Wharram Percy (previously Lesser, South or West Wharram to distinguish it from Greater, North or East Wharram, now Wharram le Street) begins in 1086 with an entry in the Domesday Book giving an assessment of nine carucates, eight in the king's own hand and one held by in return for military service by a certain Chilbert. (**30**). The entry includes the abbreviation '2M', reckoning each of the holdings a manor but not necessarily implying manor houses.

The first specific reference to a building, 'a capital messuage', is in 1254 when Peter de

30 *Some Wharram Townships in the Domesday Book (1086). From the summary. fo. 382r. In Scard Hundred; fifth line, last entry* – Warran *(Wharram-le-Street),* xii car. *(carucates); eighth line* – Touetorp *(Towthorpe),* vi c – Ibid(em) iii c. In Bredale *(Burdale),* vi c. Ibid. x bo*(bovates).*

In Hacle Hundred: 10th line – In Warron *(Wharram Percy),* ix c.; *11th line* – In Sixtendale *(Thixendale),* v c. & vi bo. Ibid. iii c. & ii bo. In Redrestorp*(Raisthorpe)* iii c. *Ibid. ii bo.* Ibid. i car.

Royal manors have the superscript Rex; *tenants in chief are similarly indicated – the count of Mortain (Wharram le Street, Towthorpe and Thixendale); Hugh son of Baldric (Burdale and Raisthorpe; and Odo Albalistarius (Thixendale and Raisthorpe).*

Percy added to his own holding at Wharram the manorial rights of a second party, Henry the Chamberlain, whose family may have been at Wharram as Percy tenants as early as 1166. It cannot therefore be determined whether each had a manor house at Wharram and who was

31 *Typical small chalk quarries, 6 ft (2 m) across by 13 ft (4 m) deep, individually dug to provide building material for the peasant houses. A bridge was left between each and the small unused rubble thrown into one quarry as the next was dug.*

building the excavated structure in the last quarter of the twelfth century. The short life of this manor house revealed by archaeology – there was pottery datable to the second half of the thirteenth century among the infill of the abandoned cellar – would seem to match the date of the unified ownership in 1254, with the building being abandoned soon after. However, this leaves open the question of whether the manor house earthworks (as yet unexcavated) at the north end of the village then replaced one in Area 10 or whether there had always been two manorial complexes, maybe as far back as the '2M' recorded in the Domesday Book.

In the later thirteenth century the area seems to have remained mainly derelict until the early fourteenth century, but a large network of quarries was dug, providing a useful source of chalk for building or lime making without destroying valuable land elsewhere (31). It was these quarries that destroyed the evidence for the timber hall and any other manorial structures. In the early fourteenth century the site was levelled and then utilized for the building of a sequence of peasant houses (33). It is this manorial connection that may make the development of Toft 10 different from the other tofts. Furthermore, the toft became exception-

32 *1969 Cambridge oblique air photograph showing in the foreground the clear earthworks of the north manor house. Beyond the fence in shadow the excavations in Area 6 are in progress, and, top left, the newly-ploughed ridge and fallow shows up as soil marks.*

ally large in the fifteenth century when 9 and 10 were thrown together and a stone wall put round the whole enclosure of toft and croft, while most crofts had simple banks with either a hedge or fence.

The north manor

The discovery of the Norman manor house was an important bonus for excavations that had been intended to be only of peasant houses. The earthworks of the second (north) manor house (32) have not been excavated, but an attempt has been made to interpret the extensive earthworks (8). The buildings across the northern end of the village appear in the twelfth century to have comprised the area of the later manor and a regular row of peasant houses (34) on its east. These seem to have been cleared away after the manors were amalgamated in 1254. If so, the buildings of peasant houses in the abandoned manor area of Tofts 9 and 10 in the early fourteenth century may not indicate intense pressure on land at a time when the village population might be expected to be stable or contracting but result simply from the need to rehouse some of the dispossessed peasants, an early example of emparking if the 'park' and 'an acre [0.4 ha] enclosed by a ditch' mentioned in a grant of 1320 lay next to the manor.

The thirteenth-century manor complex comprises four main areas, the central core having the living accommodation and main farm activities. An area to the west included a large barn. This may have been the grain storage area, although the end doors to the barn resemble many sheephouses in Yorkshire, so this could have been a sheep area. To the south there was a yard with a grain-drying kiln (35, p. 75) sensibly separated from the storage if the west building was a barn. To the east of the main manor buildings there was a through way to the open fields, its width suggesting a driveway for cattle.

The enclosure to the east, the area where there were originally peasant tofts, was left open to the valley side and contained two structures too large to be roofed, so they are likely to have been used for animals. This would give a large grazing area with open access to the valley side and the whole area may have formed the 'park' of 1320.

An interpretation of the interior earthworks would be (8): a hall with a typical cross-passage

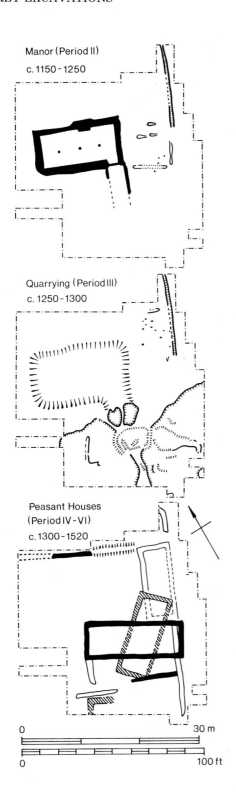

Manor (Period II)
c. 1150 - 1250

Quarrying (Period III)
c. 1250 - 1300

Peasant Houses
(Period IV - VI)
c. 1300 - 1520

0   30 m

0   100 ft

33 (left) *Area 10: three plans showing the constant changes in land use and building position in Toft 10 between the twelfth and fifteenth centuries. Following middle Saxon aristocratic occupation, a short distance to its west a stone manor house was built in the twelfth century. After the manor house was abandoned in the late thirteenth century, the area was used for quarrying (Period III). In the fourteenth and fifteenth centuries there was a sequence of peasant houses (Periods IV–VI) which were repaired and rebuilt on different alignments until the village was deserted about 1500.*

at the east end and a raised area at the west, which looks very much like the dais on which would be the table where the lord sat; and to the west of the hall a series of buildings that may have formed the solar block or the private living quarters of the Percies. It is significant that this area is closed off from the barn, with no doors in the east wall of the barn. This might suggest the area between the barn and the solar block was the private garden of the manor where plants could be grown against the east wall of the barn, protected from the prevailing west winds.

To the east of the hall would have been the service wing with buttery and pantry. The raised rectangular earthworks to the north are typical of waist-high ovens, which would be expected in the bakehouse and the brewhouse of a manor. The main entrance to the hall was from the south via an inner courtyard. The building to the north of this might have been either stables or other manorial offices. To the east of the service wing the detached building could have been the kitchen, often separated to reduce the danger of fire from cooking, joined to the service wing by an open covered passage or pentice. The round structure in the northeast of the complex is most likely to have been a dovecote. Doves were an important part of manorial diet.

Since excavations at Wharram repeatedly prove that everything is much more complicated than first expected, an excavation of this north manorial complex might show quite a different interpretation from that suggested

34 (right) *Plan of the medieval village as it may have been originally laid out with two parallel north-south Rows of tofts and crofts and a central green on the hillside closed by a west-east headrow to the north.*

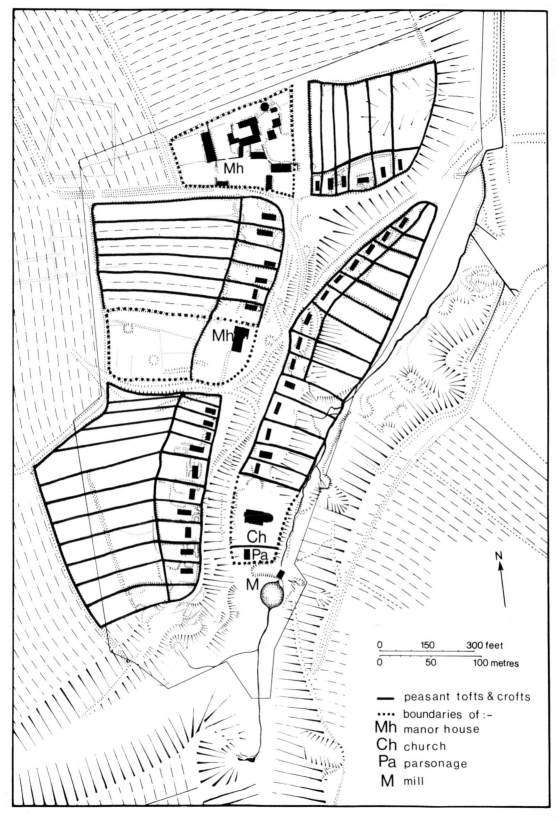

Mh

Mh

Ch
Pa

M

N

| 0 | 150 | 300 feet |
| 0 | 50 | 100 metres |

—— peasant tofts & crofts
···· boundaries of :-
Mh manor house
Ch church
Pa parsonage
M mill

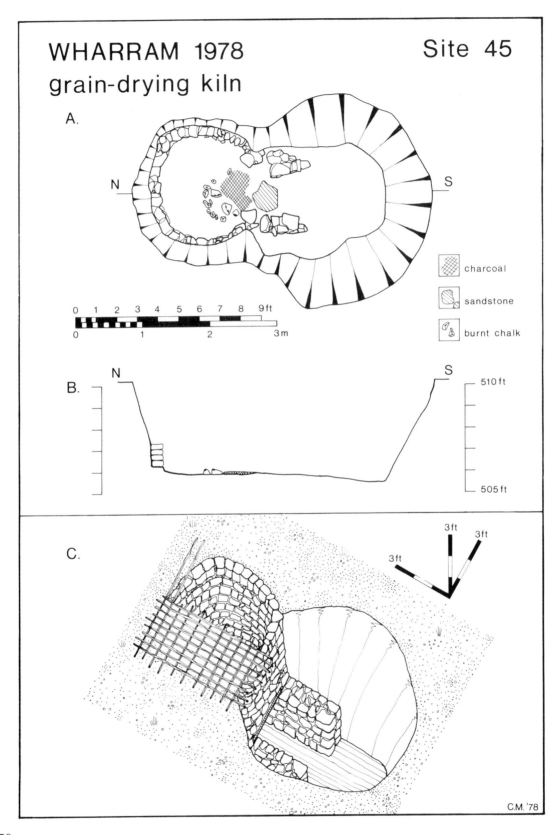

WHARRAM 1978
grain-drying kiln

Site 45

A.

N ———

——— S

0 1 2 3 4 5 6 7 8 9ft

0 1 2 3m

charcoal

sandstone

burnt chalk

B.

N

S

510 ft

505 ft

C.

3ft

3ft

3ft

C.M. '78

<50>50</50>

35 *North manor: plan of a thirteenth-century grain-drying kiln with a reconstruction drawing below. A low fire would have been lit in the stoke pit to the right and the grain for drying placed on a temporary platform to the left. Thee kilns were used for drying grain, peas, beans and other crops, and for malting. One was mentioned in the 1368 survey.*

here. Nevertheless, as the area is so large it is very unlikely ever to be excavated fully, and it seemed worthwhile to try and interpret the jumbled maze of earthworks that mean little to the visitor.

Thus there seem to be two types of manor buildings. The twelfth-century one in Area 10 apparently had just a solar block and hall and perhaps other timber buildings not found – for example, the dating of the timber buildings immediately to the east of the solar block has not been fully established. In contrast, the thirteenth-century north manor is a complex series of structures set round several court-yards.

Such a complex might seem to be late medi-eval but the very limited trial excavations produced no fourteenth-century pottery. The dates of building expenditure cannot be known as there are no manorial accounts surviving and the same deficiency conceals the nature of the farming operations conducted on the lord's behalf at the demesne farm (perhaps rep-resented by the earthworks to the south of the 'park'). The demesne is known from a document of 1323 to have consisted of 27 bovates dispersed regularly over the open fields of the township (with an area of perhaps 20 acres each (p. 47)) but with the loss of the account rolls it is impossible to know when the villagers' labour services were commuted for rents and the demesne leased out.

The last time that the manor buildings were given a positive value in a survey was in 1323. They were still standing in 1368 with a corn barn attached yet were of no value once the cost of repairs was taken into account. But farming was being actively pursued by the peasants: 68 bovates were in cultivation and the water corn mills (p. 67) are known to have been in action grinding corn in 1435 and 1458.

Documents do not indicate when the lord of the manor ceased to be resident. The Peter de Percy of 1254 was not the head of the main branch of the family from Alnwick Castle, Northumberland, and therefore might have resided at Wharram for at least some part of the year, for he had other Yorkshire properties. His son, Robert, left an insane heiress in 1321, and she and her husband unsuccessfully tried to give the manor to the newly-founded monas-tery of Haltemprice near Hull (1) in 1336; the advowson and rectory (p. 103) had been given nine years earlier.

Her son succeeded after his father had suc-cumbed to the Black Death in 1349, and on his death without heirs the manor reverted to the main branch of the Percies in 1367, saving only the interest of the widow. In the assignment of her dower the widow was granted a cottage, the 'Priesthouse', in lieu of the third of the manor house that was her due. Within ten years of her death in 1394 the indifference of the owner was shown by an exchange of the manor with a Durham family, the Hiltons, for one at Shilbottle, Northumberland. A Hilton heightened the church tower and decorated it with his coat of arms but he probably never resided here, for surveys of 1435 and 1458 simply recorded 'the site of a manor' with no valuation, and it was a member of that family who was accused in 1517 of evicting four households.

3

Official recognition

It was in 1960 that the first conscious effort was made to study wider aspects of the village. Although research funds were still not available, the number of volunteers who were prepared to come and excavate for three weeks each year had increased. On a national scale there were several major village research projects in progress, and the Ministry of Works had initiated rescue excavations all over the country, which were rapidly building up a good series of medieval peasant house types and sequences.

Work had started in 1955 on a clay site at Wolfhampcote, Warwicks. (5) to try to contrast the results with a stone site like Wharram, but results were so poor that it was clear this type of site could not be excavated without large research funds, so it was decided that Wharram, rather than another site, should remain the research excavation of the Deserted Medieval Village Research Group. With the increased labour it would be possible to excavate a second site concurrently with Area 6.

The parish church

Two factors led to the decision to excavate the parish church of St Martin. Firstly, any second excavation would have to be in an area not grazed, since the two fields with the main village earthworks were grazed by a tenant farmer who would not have allowed a second large area on the plateau to be excavated concurrently. At this time the only possible area was the church. Although the church had been gradually decaying during the 1950s, following the last service in 1949, archaeological attention was entirely concentrated on the medieval peasant house excavations, which had been started as a reaction to what was thought to be too much emphasis on churches and manor houses.

Secondly, in 1959 the west wall of the church tower collapsed. When the rubble was being cleared up, it was apparent that the whole church fabric was at risk. As the plaster was peeling from the walls various different periods of stonework became visible, and the realization dawned that here was an opportunity, rare in Britain, of investigating a complete parish church both above and below ground, together with a sample area of the churchyard in which to study aspects of the medieval population. Negotiations with the church authorities therefore took place. The first faculty, giving permission to excavate, was granted in 1962, and the work was continued until 1974.

By that time the whole future of Wharram and the research project had fundamentally changed. From the start of the work of the Deserted Medieval Village Research Group in 1952 visits to new deserted medieval villages, which were discovered all over the country, showed that many of these were being levelled and ploughed as part of the great post-war programme of increasing arable land. By the early 1960s almost all the sites known had been visited by Hurst and Beresford, and it was possible to select the most important deserted medieval villages in the country that might be preserved. In 1965 a Memorandum was presented to the Ministry of Public Building and Works (as it had then become) recommending the preservation of the 50 best deserted medieval villages in the country and suggesting that the best six should be taken into Guardianship. In 1967 the Ancient Monuments Board, under the chairmanship of Sir Mortimer Wheeler, visited Wharram Percy and commended the proposals. The Ministry of Public Building and Works then approached both the Church Commissioners, in respect of the church, and Lord Middleton, as owner of the village site, and both readily agreed.

After lengthy negotiations the parish church of St Martin was placed in the care of the Ministry of Public Building and Works in 1972 and, by the generosity of the 11th Baron Middleton, the whole 38-acre (15.4-ha) deserted medieval village site was placed in care by the Birdsall Estates Company in 1974. This immediately transformed the project. Following on from the voluntary work of the first 20 years, it was now possible to plan a second 20-year programme carried out in conjunction with the Department of the Environment, the former Ministry of Public Building and Works. For the first time public funds were available and these were initially used to consolidate the church. Work started on making the walls secure in 1970, in anticipation of the church being placed in Guardianship, and was completed in 1977. As the main aim of the Department of the Environment was to have a site for presentation to the public, a 20-year programme was drawn up to excavate a selected series of different aspects of the site and mark them out for display.

One effect of all this on the archaeological programme was that it was now possible for work to be carried out anywhere in the village rather than being limited to one site at a time. However, the most important effect was the possibility of paying professional supervisors rather than having to rely on a changing body of volunteers: several excavations could thus be directed simultaneously, with the hope of the same person carrying each project through to publication. As Wharram Percy became well known in the archaeological circle it became more attractive to students, and it was now possible to provide free food for volunteers who had experience and so ensure a larger regular labour force.

The ten-year programme for the 1970s envisaged, firstly, the completion of the excavation and survey of the parish church and sample areas of the churchyard. Secondly, work on the terrace would be extended to an excavation of the sequence of dams south of the church and the medieval and post-medieval parsonages north of it. Thirdly, most importantly as it turned out, there was to be a programme of selected trenches through the boundary earthworks all round the village, since previous work had been limited to single areas. The site was then to be put in context by Parish Surveys of Wharram Percy and Wharram le Street.

In this chapter the work on the church and the mill will be described, together with the trial trenches dug to determine the dates of the boundary earthworks and the general development of the topography of the village. This work led to a considerable widening of the questions asked and a major new programme in the 1980s, which is the subject of Chapter 4. A discussion of the Parish Surveys follows in Chapter 5 and the study of the village after desertion in Chapter 6.

The parish church dedicated to St Martin stands on a terrace in the valley, close to the stream that runs near the eastern boundary of the churchyard. Its unusual and semi-isolated position has never been explained, although the isolation was less in the Middle Ages when the houses of the eastern Row (34) extended as far as the vicarage, which adjoined the church. The eastern side of the valley is here at its steepest, but on the west the ground slopes up to the terrace before rising to the plateau where the nearest houses (Area 6) were to be found. There is evidence that in the past the terrace was artificially extended towards the stream.

The earliest documentary reference to the church is no earlier than one naming the vicar, Ive, datable to 1210–20, and the next is that of 1254 recording Peter de Percy's acquisition of the right to nominate the incumbent when a living fell vacant. There are no documentary references to its structure before a gift for the rood loft in 1531 and a succession of complaints about the decay of the chancel from 1555 onwards.

When Beresford first visited the church in 1948 it was in poor repair but still occasionally used. Until Thixendale acquired its own church in 1870 there was some incentive to keep its fabric in some state of repair but thereafter its condition deteriorated, and the last major work was in 1923. Burials ceased in 1906 and the last marriage was solemnized in 1928. Services were held in the summer months of each year till August 1941 and were resumed after the Second World War, but no service was held from 1949 until 1982 when an annual service began to be organized during the excavations. After 1949 decay was rapid (36a and b), the fittings were removed, slates were dislodged by winter storms and roosting pigeons, and the badly cracked west face of the tower collapsed in a storm in December 1959.

On the Continent there have been many excavations inside surviving churches and there is a wide corpus of comparative material. In England there have always been difficulties in excavating churches in use, so only a handful

37 (above) *View from the west of excavation in progress at the east end of the nave showing the massive foundations for the late Saxon Period II stone church. To the left are nineteenth-century burials.*

36a (left) *General 1954 view of the inside of the church looking east after the pews had been removed. The ceiling was starting to collapse after the loss of slates admitted the rain.*

36b (left) *General 1954 view of the inside of the church looking west. The font, left, and the wall memorials, right, were still in place.*

have been excavated even now. In 1960 this was a very rare occurrence indeed except for limited work when repairs were in progress. Despite the fact that the study of religious buildings was very popular in the nineteenth century it comprised mainly excavation of monastic sites with only very general studies of the standing structure of the normal parish church. In particular very little was known about the earliest periods of most churches. Examination of the structure of churches might lead to the conclusion that the fabric was Norman or later. It was likely, however, that with archaeological investigation earlier evidence would come to light.

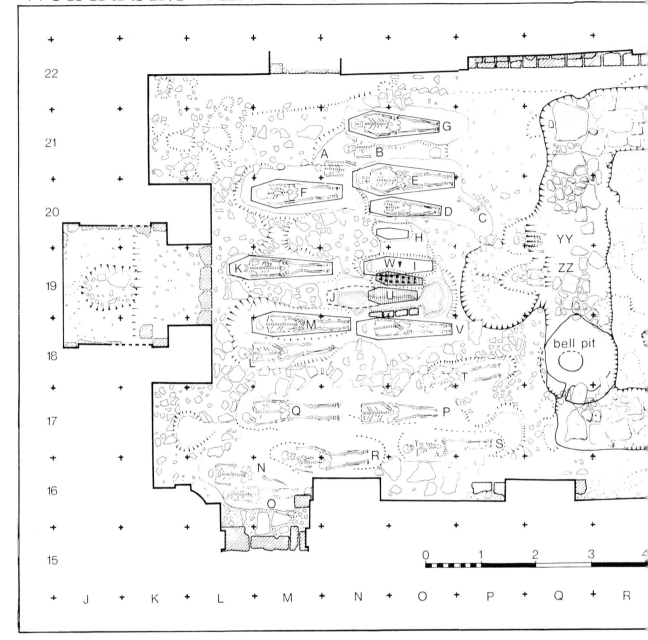

38 *Detailed excavation plan of the nave of the church showing the foundations of the late Saxon churches and the disturbance caused by the many post-medieval burials.*

In the 1950s the Royal Commission on Historical Monuments had surveyed Wharram Percy church, identifying six main periods of construction. At this time the plaster on the walls was still intact, but by 1960 much of it had peeled off with the damp so that closer analysis was possible and further construction phases were immediately recognizable.

In 1962 the period of public funding had not yet begun, and because of the continued voluntary nature of the labour force the church had to be excavated in a series of small areas (**37**), many of them directed by different supervisors. It was not until the final seasons that a more co-ordinated approach was possible,

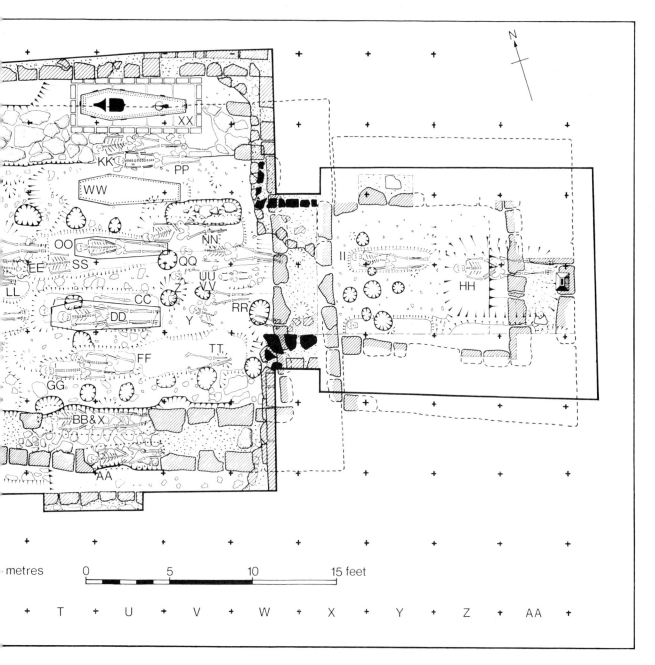

metres 0 5 10 15 feet

+ T + U + V + W + X + Y + Z + AA +

culminating in the excavation of an area to the west of the church in 1972, the area south of the chancel in 1973 and the final reopening of the whole of the nave in 1974 (**38** and **colour plate 4**). The report was published in 1987.

No evidence emerged for the building of an Anglian church on the terrace before the late-ninth-century Scandinavian invasions as had been hoped from the findings of the eight- and ninth-century coins and sculpture. A series of post-holes may have formed the foundations for the earliest church on this site, built of timber in the tenth century (Period I). This was followed by a small two-celled stone church, comprising a rectangular nave and chancel, which is likely to have been built in the late tenth or early eleventh centuries (Period II). In view of its isolation from the main Saxon occupation on the plateau and its small size, this is likely to have been not the parish church but rather

39 *A conjectural reconstruction model of the church in the twelfth century with large nave, chancel and apsidal east end, viewed from the north.*

a private church built by one of the late Saxon lords.

The parish of Wharram Percy may have been formed in the middle of the twelfth century, with the large Period-III church built then to provide accommodation for the parishioners, who would previously have worshipped in a series of small churches, similar to Period II at Wharram, scattered over the area. These changes may also have been linked with the final planning of the village (p. 84). The new church was two-celled, like Period II, but on a much larger scale with a nave and apsidal east end (**39** and **colour plate 2**), built on a large chalk raft extending the width of the terrace. A large west tower was planned but abandoned in Period IV possibly due to foundation problems, for the Normans were not aware that they were building over an earlier quarry that had provided construction material for the first stone church. A much smaller tower was built

in a most unusual position, half in and half out of the west end of the nave. This was still not secure due to unsafe foundations, and gave constant problems over the centuries, culminating in the collapse in 1959.

Period V, in the later twelfth century, saw a large south aisle built along the full length of the nave and beyond, with an arcade of round-headed Norman arches. In the thirteenth century (Period VI) there was further major expansion of the accommodation for both people and new altars with the construction of a small, two-bay north aisle with pointed arches, the squaring off of the east end of the chancel, a new wide chancel arch and the building of a porch in the second bay of the south side (**44**).

After this steady period of expansion during the time of increasing population and prosperity there was only one further major addition to the church, the Period VII north-east chapel in the early fourteenth century (**42**). The chancel arch was narrowed, then in the fifteenth century the Hiltons added a new battlemented upper storey to the tower decor-

40 *General 1964 view of the excavations to the north-east of the standing church showing to the left foundations of the long medieval chancels supported on an artificial chalk raft built out into the valley and, on the right, the north-east chapel.*

41 *View from the south-west in 1964 of the excavated foundations of the medieval chancels showing the semi-circular twelfth-century apse (Period IV) and the squared-off thirteenth-century east end (Period VI).*

ated with their arms. However, the decline soon set in with the reduction of the length of the south aisle in Period VIII. With the lower fifteenth-century population, and the final depopulation of Wharram Percy about 1500, both the aisles and the chapel were demolished in Period IX and the chancel made smaller in the seventeenth century.

This interpretation of the development of the parish church (**43, 44**) has to rest solely on the archaeological and architectural evidence, for there is little medieval documentary evidence.

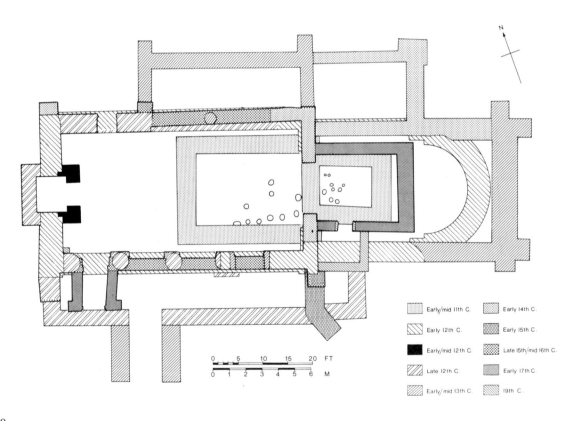

Early/mid 11th C.		Early 14th C.	
Early 12th C.		Early 15th C.	
Early/mid 12th C.		Late 15th/mid 16th C.	
Late 12th C.		Early 17th C	
Early/mid 13th C.		19th C.	

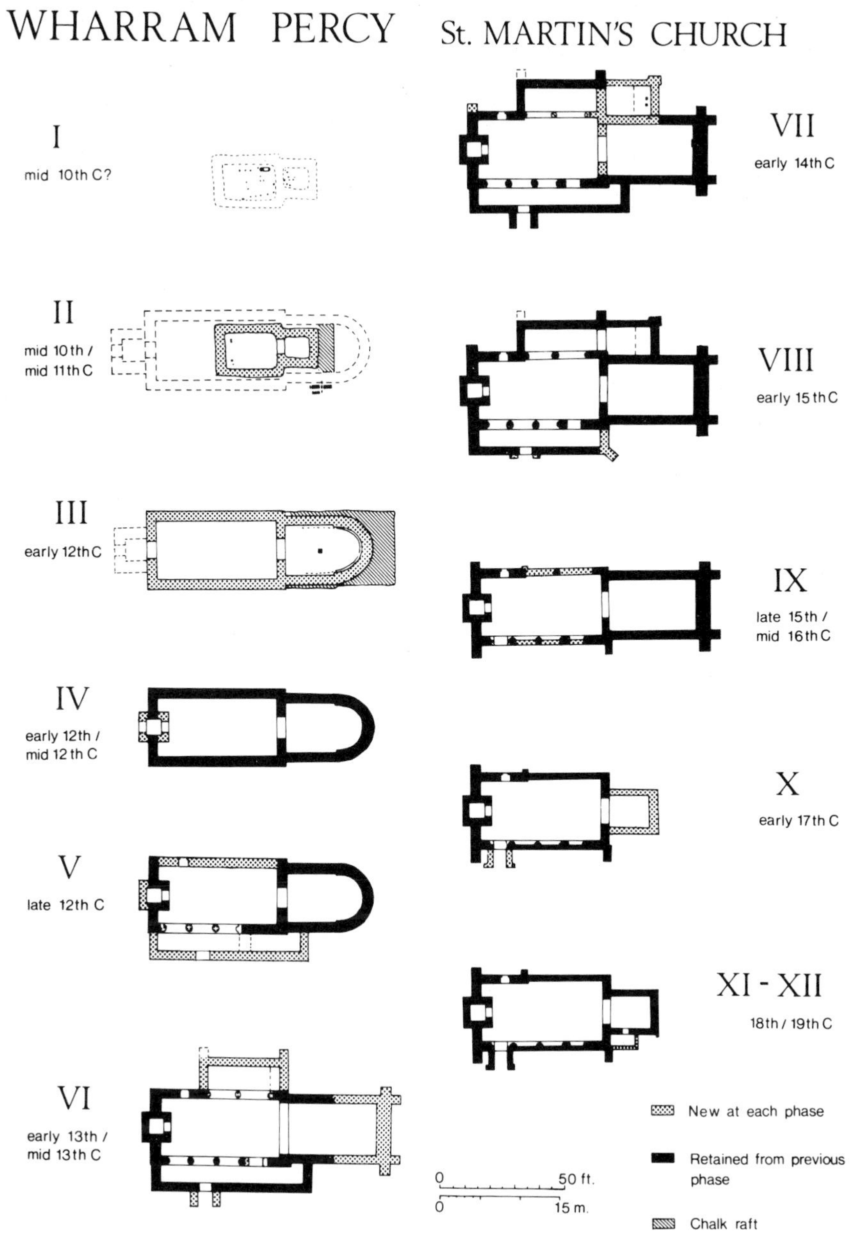

WHARRAM PERCY St. MARTIN'S CHURCH

I
mid 10th C?

II
mid 10th /
mid 11th C

III
early 12th C

IV
early 12th /
mid 12th C

V
late 12th C

VI
early 13th /
mid 13th C

VII
early 14th C

VIII
early 15th C

IX
late 15th /
mid 16th C

X
early 17th C

XI - XII
18th / 19th C

New at each phase

Retained from previous phase

Chalk raft

0   50 ft.
0   15 m.

42 (top left)   *A conjectural reconstruction model of the church, at it greatest extent in the fourteenth century, with the addition of a north aisle, north-east chapel and the east end squared off, viewed from the north.*

43 (bottom left)   *Excavation plan of the church showing the complex series of wall foundations interpreted in a chronological sequence.*

44 (Above)   *An interpretation plan showing the different periods separately, starting with the small private tenth- and eleventh-century churches (Periods I and II), followed by the large twelfth-century parochial church (Periods III and IV), with aisles and chapels added (Periods V–VII), and then the gradual reduction in size of the church (Periods VIII–XII) as various settlements in the parish became deserted and the population decreased.*

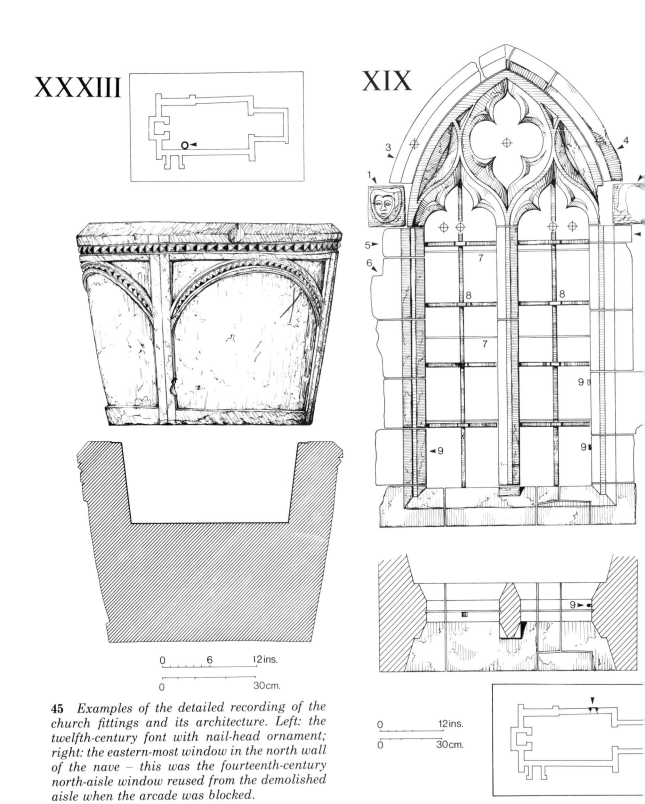

XXXIII

XIX

45 *Examples of the detailed recording of the church fittings and its architecture. Left: the twelfth-century font with nail-head ornament; right: the eastern-most window in the north wall of the nave – this was the fourteenth-century north-aisle window reused from the demolished aisle when the arcade was blocked.*

The acquisition of the advowson by the Percies in 1254, the period between 1308 an 1322 when a Percy was rector, the interest of the Scropes between 1322 and the transfer of the advowson to Haltemprice Priory in 1327 might each suggest a period of special interest in the church leading to building or major repairs, but it is very hard to link any of these to architectural phases except possibly the early-fourteenth-century north-east chapel, which may have been built to house the altar for the chantry endowed by Sir Geoffrey le Scrope in 1326–7.

The combination of the archaeological with the architectural (**45**) evidence was, however, a major feature of the study of the church. It was possible to investigate the various building periods by examining the wall elevations to augment the evidence of the changing founda-

tions. It demonstrated how little of the complex story of a building can be worked out if the walls have been demolished to ground level.

The inside south wall of the church is a good example (**46**). The upper part of the wall is ashlar, with neat courses of sandstone blocks, added during the twelfth-century major rebuilding of the church. High in the wall towards the left end an original window survives, blocked up. In the middle, disturbed stonework suggests the original position of another. Into and through this wall were inserted the rounded arches of the late-twelfth-century south aisle. These in turn were blocked up about 1500, when they were filled with reused early-fifteenth-century windows from the aisle, which had just been demolished. To the left the doorway into the south aisle reuses earlier architectural fragments, including chevron-decorated voussoirs from the twelfth-century round-headed chancel arch, put together to form a pointed arch, which would have been more fashionable in the thirteenth century. The window in this blocked doorway was rebuilt in 1923 following

46 *Elevation drawing of the inside of the south wall of the church showing the complex development of a single wall.*

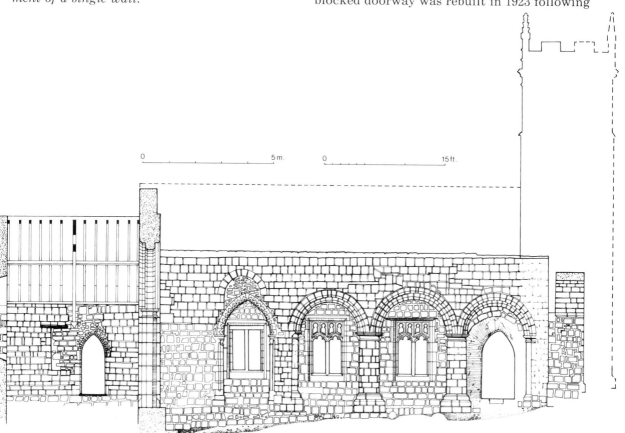

the partial collapse of the outer face of the south wall. A similar complex sequence can be worked out from most of the other walls.

The churchyard

The second part of the project on the church sampled parts of the churchyard to obtain a series of burials to study the skeletons of a medieval rural population. It was fortunate that a number of grave slabs covering the burials of late-Saxon lords of the eleventh

century survived in the churchyard in the south-east angle between the chancel and the nave. More of these were disturbed by the twelfth-century Norman builders who used them as foundations for the south aisle. These slabs were decorated with simple ribs and one with a simple cross (**colour plate 7**). One covered a child burial. The slabs had head- and footstones but, as these had been cut off at ground level, it is not known if they were carved.

No medieval grave slabs remain *in situ*, but many fragments are built into the walls, especially on the south side. These include complex foliated crosses with swords that denote men at arms, presumably members of the family of the lords of the manor. Another had a chalice and a book and would have covered the grave of a priest (**47**). Two of the medieval burials that had chalices with them, and one with a paten as well (**colour plate 8**),

47 *A selection of grave slabs used to cover and mark burials. Left: eleventh-century grave slab of a lord with a simple rib and a cross; centre: thirteenth-century grave slab of a priest with a foliated cross and the representation of a chalice and a book; right: fourteenth-century grave slab, with a more ornate foliated cross, reconstructed from three fragments found built into the walls of the church.*

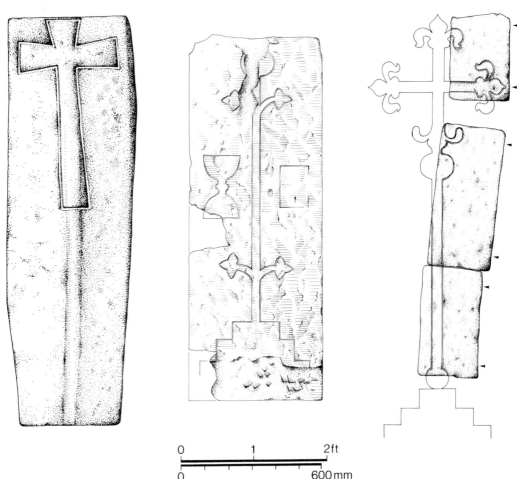

```
0            1            2ft
|────────────|────────────|

0                        600mm
```

48 *Close-up view of some of the medieval burials to the west of the church. Across the centre are the stone slabs covering conduit supply water to the farm (probably c. 1775).*

can also be interpreted as the burials of priests. The later-medieval builders had as little interest in preserving these grave markers as did their twelfth-century predecessors.

Burials had much disturbed the inside of the nave (**37**) and it was fortunate that they had not destroyed all evidence for the pre-Norman churches. Most of these graves were post-medieval and of quite late date. There were no burials under the pews so earlier foundations were preserved in these areas. The burials were much more numerous up the central aisle and behind the pews at the west end of the church.

In the graveyard itself the area to the south of the church, where burial continued until the early twentieth century, was not available for investigation, but it was possible to excavate two sample areas to the north and west of the church where burials ceased after the desertion of the village in the early sixteenth century.

About 600 burials were excavated, comprising about 1,000 individuals. There were several superimposed layers of graves, and many earlier burials had been disturbed by later ones. The graves were regularly laid out in rows, and the graveyard seems to have been used for at least four cycles of burial as the ground level had built up, especially on the north side. To the west the depth of soil was less (**48**). All this material is still being worked on, but it is hoped that it will produce important evidence for the physical anthropology, mortality, disease and nutrition of a medieval rural population to compare with evidence from urban populations in York.

The mill and fishpond

The stream, simply named the Beck, which runs along the bottom of the valley to the east of the village below the plateau and the terrace, has its source in a series of seven springs that emerge from the junction of the clay and the chalk. The first of these springs lies just south of the junction of Deep Dale and Drue Dale, leaving both dry in their upper parts except in the wettest times of the year and during major storms when water emerges along the valleys further south. From at least Bronze-Age times, and possibly the Neolithic period, this large supply of water must have made this 650-yd (600-m) length of valley a preferred site for settlement with the special facility of providing plenty of water for animals and easy access up the valley side to the grazing areas on the plateau.

The area where the stream had been dammed just south of the churchyard was excavated between 1972 and 1981. The aim was to see how the stream had been utilized and to obtain environmental evidence from the waterlogged deposits, since this does not survive in the chalk areas of the rest of the site. In this ten-

year programme a very complicated sequence was found in the valley bottom. There was no evidence here of any prehistoric or Roman activity, but in the Saxon period there seems to have been some initial damming, possibly connected with fishing.

From the late Saxon and early medieval period a complex sequence of low clay dams, cut by a series of channels and with the front strengthened with wattle hurdling, was found (**49**). These are thought to have been part of a horizontal-wheel water mill, and indeed several padstones were discovered around the eroded remains of a wheel pit: these traces may well be the only remains of the late-Saxon mill. To judge from the number of fragments of millstones found it must have been nearby. Remains of both plaster beetles and furniture beetles suggested structures nearby, but these may have been washed away or removed after the mill was abandoned. A series of channels through the dams were found: these clearly had to be renewed frequently, resulting in a sequence of at least five major phases.

49 *Isometric drawing of the sequence of small dams for the late-Saxon and early-medieval horizontal wheel watermill. The dam and some of the silts from the pond containing water-logged deposits were sealed by the large fourteenth-century dam for the fishpond.*

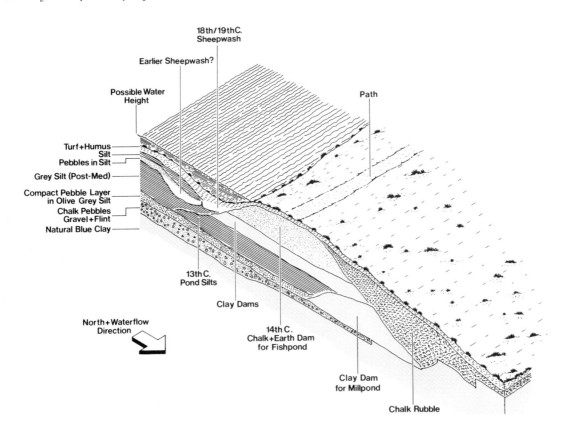

In the thirteenth century two mills are recorded; a north mill and a south mill. These are likely to have been water mills for grinding corn for the two Chamberlain and Percy Manors. The site of the north mill is not known but it is likely to have been opposite the north manor and may have been destroyed when the railway was built, while the excavated south mill would have been related to the Area 10 Manor house. By the thirteenth century the Saxon mill became derelict. The dam was then heightened, and it is possible that milling still continued, as the documents suggest. A much larger chalk-rubble dam was built across the valley in the fourteenth century, apparently to retain a fishpond rather than a mill pond. Thanks to this dam, major sections of the earlier dams were sealed with pond silt in front (**49**). All the rest of the evidence had been cleared away during subsequent clearing out of the fishpond and later construction.

After 1254, when the two manors were amalgamated, only one mill would have been required, and it is significant that in 1368 there was a *Milndam* (mill dam) to the north of the village and a pool to the south. The north corn mill therefore survived in use, but the south mill was converted into a fishpond, possibly by Haltemprice Priory (**1**) who were given the millpool in the 1320s. The excavation suggested that both the dam and the pond required regular maintenance, with a series of temporary channels being dug through the dam during work on its repair and periodic heightening. This fishpond remained in use, at least as a pond, after the desertion of the village. The dam was refaced with sandstone blocks in the eighteenth century by either the parson or the farmer. In the nineteenth century a sheep-wash was built against the dam. This was in turn abandoned by 1935 when the Norton Rural District Council built a water collection tank, drawing off water from the springs to pump it away for domestic use. The sheep-wash was replaced *c.* 1927 by a concrete sheep-dip on the west side of Nut Wood, utilizing the stream lower down (**2**). Now the pump house has been abandoned in its turn, and the stream simply flows through the valley with the fourteenth-century dam and fishpond

recreated for the general public to see (**50** and **front cover**).

In the main part of the village, on the plateau, where the sub-soil is chalk, the only artefacts surviving are pottery, metal, bone and stone. These were, however, only a small selection of the objects of daily life, so if one relies only on this area the archaeological picture is a very restricted one. In the waterlogged conditions in the valley, and particularly in the silt layers of the early-medieval pond sealed by the fourteenth-century fishpond dam above, a much wider range of objects survived. Besides the structural wattles, these comprised wooden objects (including part of a shovel blade), fragments of leather shoes, a larger (so far unidentified) object of leather, basketry and textiles.

Also preserved was pollen, the evidence from which suggests that there were, in the early-medieval period, no trees in the immediate vicinity of the pond and that there was a mixed arable and grass landscape. Other evidence includes beetles and actual fragments of plants, which all help to build up a picture of the ecology of the village about the time of the Norman Conquest. This waterlogged material, together with fragments of charcoal from other archaeological deposits, gives us knowledge

50 *General view of the reconstructed fourteenth-century fishpond with the ruined church and churchyard beyond, under the snow.*

about a wide range of trees that were growing elsewhere at Wharram at this time (p. 127). Other burnt material from various parts of the village includes seeds, showing the types of cereals grown and some of the weeds which grew amongst the crops. Unfortunately this random selection of material is not necessarily typical, so it is not possible to tell what proportions of different crops were being planted. Nevertheless it does fill out considerably the information obtained from the more usual, largely indestructible, archaeological finds.

Boundaries

The excavation of the manor house, church and mill dam were planned to extend the investigation of the medieval village beyond the first objective of studying the medieval peasant house and daily life of the village. Once the whole range of earthworks was available for unhampered study a ten-year programme took place on the plateau, trial trenching the boundaries of the tofts and crofts to determine when the village was laid out and how it developed. It was this work, with its exciting and unexpected results, that led to the widening of the questions to be asked in the 1980s.

Between 1971 and 1980, 25 trenches were excavated round the boundaries of the site, starting in the south, moving round the west and finishing in the north. It was expected that there might be some complexity, for a trial trench cut in 1961 through the south wall of the hall of the north manor house had produced a large number of Iron-Age and Romano-British features, including a skeleton, but perversely no dating evidence for the manor house. What was completely unexpected was the discovery of archaeological features and pottery in every trench, for one of the first worries had been whether it would be possible to date boundaries that were so far away from the medieval peasant houses and their expected range of occupation debris.

In 1971 there was a simplistic view that the settlement started on the terrace by the water supply, where the Saxon church was built, spread up on to the west plateau in the twelfth century with the expansion of population and the building of the manor house in Area 10 and then further expanded to its northern limit with the building of the north manor house after the amalgamation of Percy and Chamberlain manors in 1254 and the further laying out of peasant house tofts and crofts. Thereafter,

it was thought, the village declined following the Black Death in 1349. Its houses were progressively abandoned until the final evictions about 1500 with the change from arable to sheep.

With hindsight more could have been made of understanding the church if opportunities had been grasped in the 1950s. Similarly, the right questions might have been asked of the village layout and boundaries if the implications of the 1961 discovery of not just a few fragments of pottery but a very intense premedieval occupation under the north manor house had been initially spotted. It is likely that the disappointment of not obtaining any dating evidence for the manor house was the overriding consideration. Even more surprising is the fact that the crop-mark of one of the north-west enclosures of the Iron-Age pattern of settlement (52) was clearly visible in the first oblique air photograph taken in 1948 but was not noticed (4).

The main results of the boundary trial trenches were to show that, in general terms, the main medieval earthworks were on the same alignments as Iron-Age or Romano-British boundaries that were found underneath them (52) and that there were Romano-British farms on the south-west and northern boundaries of the medieval village. Most surprising of all, was the discovery, in 1975, of an eighth-century Saxon hut on the north-east village boundary, not only 160 yd (150 m) east of a possible early settlement under the north manor (p. 71) but remote by 490 yd (450 m) from the church that had been the supposed centre of a Saxon village (54). This Saxon *Grubenhaus* was dug 20 in. (50 cm) into the ground, and had an upright post at each end, which would have been supported by a ridge pole.

The original thesis of the village starting by the church, and then spreading out with the increase of population, had been rapidly undermined during the early 1970s, but it was the finding of the *Grubenhaus* that finally revealed how complex was the story of the development of Wharram. Thus the second decade of the joint Medieval Village Research Group and Department of the Environment programme between 1980 and 1990 completely changed the concept of the project from its intermediate stage, when it tried to study as many different aspects of the medieval village as possible, to an attempt to try and understand the total landscape history of the area.

4

Wider questions

The trial trenches of the 1970s helped to formulate and define new questions for the 1980s and identify where excavation might be most productive. The programme was aimed at the completion of aspects of the medieval village by excavating the medieval parsonage, which for logistical reasons had not been available for excavation in the 1970s; investigating the prehistoric and Roman antecedents of the village (**53**); and establishing the extent of the Saxon occupation and the date of the village plan. Finally it would move on to excavate the post-medieval parsonage and the 1770s Improvers Farm, trying to link the latter to the desertion of the village about 1500, and identifying the centre from which the sixteenth- and seventeenth-century sheep farm was run. This chapter will deal with the antecedents of the medieval village, Chapter 6 with the parsonages and post-desertion farms.

In the 1980s it was possible to increase the total labour force for each three-week season up to peaks of 100 or more, not only because volunteers were still prepared to come for free food with no wages but also because Philip Rahtz was appointed the first Professor of Archaeology at York in 1979 and became associate director of excavations. With extra help from the York students, together with others from the University of Lancaster in the mid 1980s and an increasing number of foreign students, it was possible to excavate six different sites each season (**51**).

The search for the origins of Wharram was based on two main projects on the west plateau, supplemented by a series of smaller excavations round the periphery extending the original boundary trial trenches. The first west plateau excavation comprised a long, wide 55- × 11-yd (50- × 10-m) trench across the south courtyard of the north manor house. The second excavation was in the western half of Area 10, where a series of 33-ft (10-m) squares was dug with linking trenches to the surrounding earth-works. Additionally, in preparation for the programme of landscape tree-planting round the edge of the village outside the main boundaries (p. 78), six large rectangles were excavated to follow up the settlement evidence produced by the trial excavations at the boundaries. A further one was being completed in the final 1989 and 1990 seasons.

The north manor trench

The York University trench, starting in the north manor and with a new 33-ft (10-m) square excavated every two years, was designed south of an earlier 30-ft (9.1-m) square that lay immediately south of the supposed medieval hall, where extensive early occupation had been found in 1961. This was linked to the south boundary bank of the manorial enclosure and cut across the sunken road. Despite the considerable amount of excavation on deserted medieval villages over the last 30 years, this was the first time that a major 33-ft (10-m) section had been cut across a road. The trench then took in the northern half of Toft 17 to find out if the pre-medieval occupation extended across the road and whether there were any outbuildings at the back of Building 17 similar to those found in Toft 10.

This trench was most successful in showing extensive occupation from prehistoric times onwards. A scatter of Neolithic and Bronze-Age flints suggested early occupation nearby. It showed that the sunken road was laid out in the Iron Age, slightly to the north of its present line, with a series of rectangular enclosures both north and south forming a ladder pattern. The full extent of these has been discovered by geophysical survey (see **52**) showing a major east-west axis in contrast to the north-south medieval alignment. Further trial trenching has shown that the major enclosures were late Iron Age with modifications in the Roman period. In what was later to be the south courtyard of the north manor house, a large

51 *1984 oblique air photograph taken from the north during the excavation season in July, showing the earthworks as parchmarks in a dry season and the tents for the diggers on the top right. The excavations show the main projects in progress in the 1980s. At the bottom can be seen the southern part of the trench across the main west to east road. The Roman grain-drying kiln (56 and 57) may clearly be seen in the middle of the 10-m square under excavation. In the centre is one of the 33-ft (10-m) squares to the west of Area 10 where the middle-Saxon settlement was being excavated. Towards the top are the marked-out buildings in Area 6 and to the right the excavation of the Romano-British farm, which had led to the kink in the west boundary of the village when this was laid out. On the terrace, top left, are the excavations on the eighteenth-century Improving farm; the medieval and post-medieval vicarages; and beyond the ruined parish church the reconstructed fourteenth-century fishpond.*

defensive Iron-Age ditch was found with a gateway. This suggests that the main part of an aristocratic Iron-Age settlement lay underneath the later north manor house.

Occupation continued through the Roman period with evidence for the timber buildings of Romano-British farms, at first utilizing the earlier earthworks and then in the third or fourth centuries AD modifying them. In Toft 17 a sequence of late-Roman grain-drying kilns

52 *Geophysical survey plot of the north half of the medieval village site showing a major west-east axis based on the main through road. The complex comprises a series of small enclosures to north and south of the road forming a ladder pattern. The basic layout has been shown by excavation to be late Iron Age with modifications in the late Roman period. The two large enclosures to the south formed a basis for medieval crofts, which, in contrast to the Iron Age enclosure, were laid out on north-south lines, except for the head-row.*

was found, starting with a simple T-shaped kiln (**56**), replaced by a more complicated kiln of tuning-fork shape (**57**). This is important, for it suggests that cereal production was not, as might be expected, decreasing in the late-Roman period, since the later kiln had a larger capacity. Tantalizingly, it was faced with large tooled sandstone blocks from a major stone building. In view of the unlikelihood of such large stones being transported the long distance from either of the two Wharram le Street Roman villas (p. 92), there is a distinct possibility that there was a third villa at Wharram Percy, but no trace of this has so far been found in the various trial trenches cut in the vicinity to test the hypothesis. The presence of Romano-British structures both north and south of the road is no longer surprising in view of the geophysical evidence for enclosures set out on both sides in a ladder pattern.

In the Saxon period two *Grubenhäuser* were dug into the sunken road (**58**). To the north, in the enclosure that was to become the north

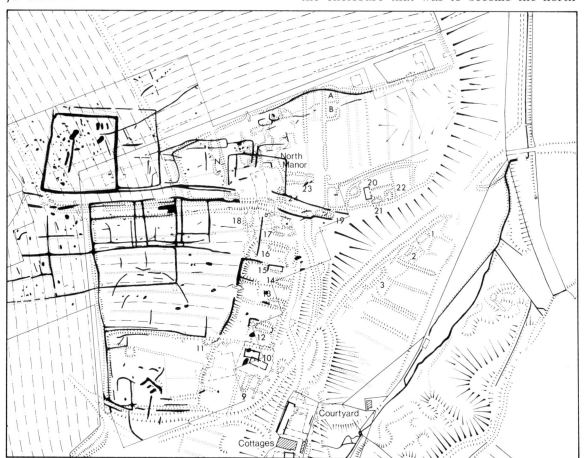

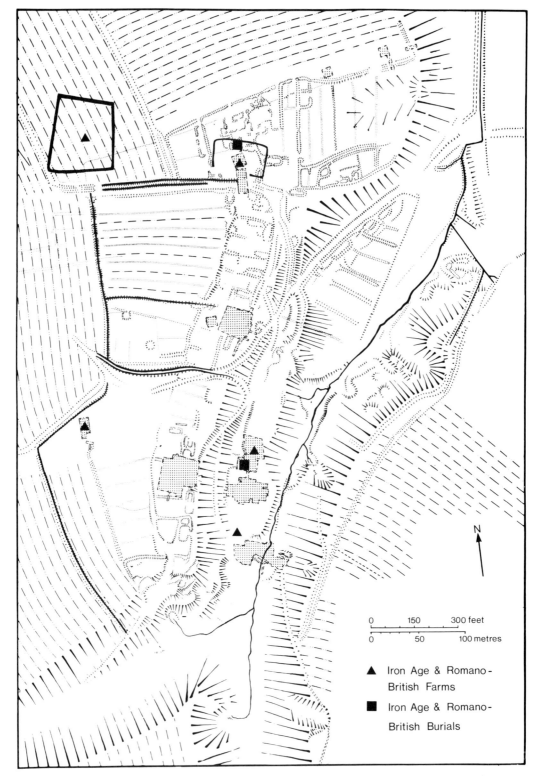

53 *Iron-Age and Roman Wharram Percy: plan showing the position of the main boundaries, the five farms and the two burials.*

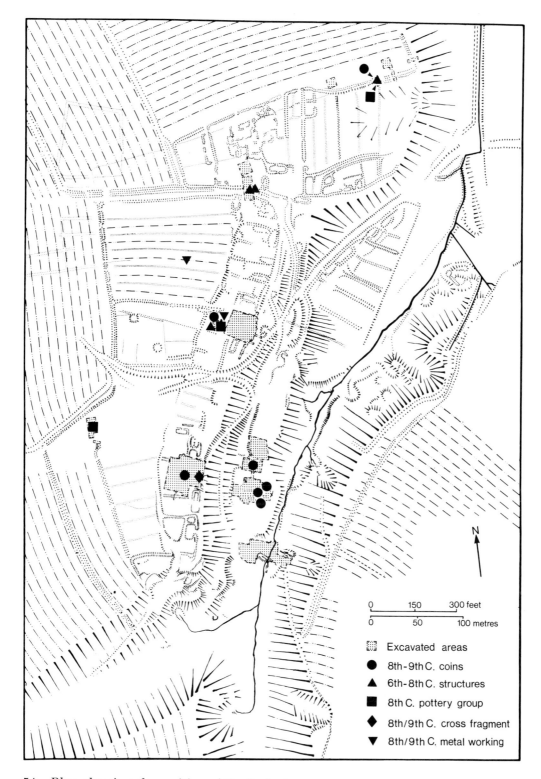

0   150   300 feet
0   50   100 metres

▦   Excavated areas
●   8th–9th C. coins
▲   6th–8th C. structures
■   8th C. pottery group
◆   8th/9th C. cross fragment
▼   8th/9th C. metal working

54 *Plan showing the position of the finds datable to the middle Saxon period between AD 650 and 850 on the site that was later to become the planned medieval village. Six different foci have been found.*

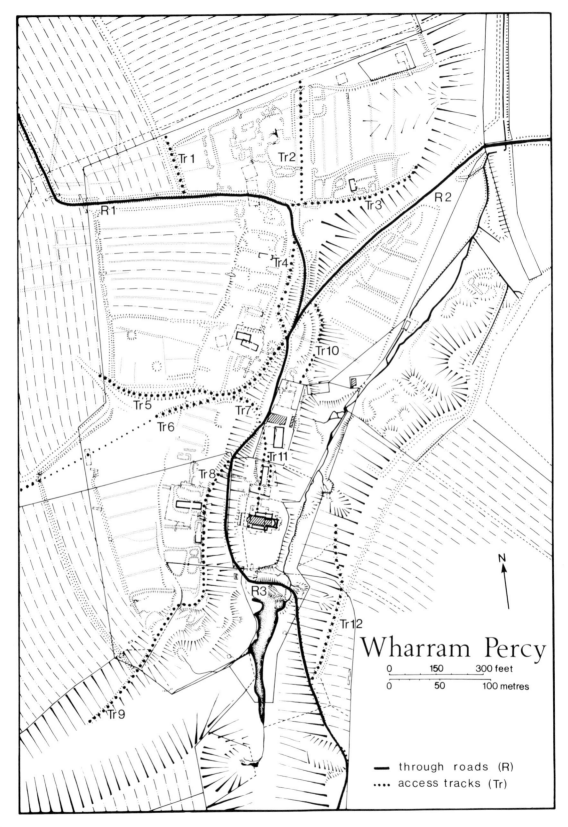

Tr 1

Tr 2

Tr 3

R 1

R 2

Tr 4

Tr 10

Tr 5

Tr 7

Tr 6

Tr 11

Tr 8

R 3

Tr 12

Tr 9

N

Wharram Percy

0   150   300 feet

0   50   100 metres

— through roads (R)

···· access tracks (Tr)

55 (left) *Roads and tracks in the village, showing the main network of through roads and access tracks. R1 was the main east-west road to the market town of Malton, R2 led to the village of Towthorpe, while R3 went to Thixendale. The tracks gave extra access from the valley to the plateau and out into the open fields.*

medieval manor, post-holes were found from a series of timber buildings that were post-Roman and pre-medieval but not closely datable from the evidence in the small areas excavated. At least one of the huts was sixth century, with a characteristic iron strike-a-light, an iron tool to make fire by being struck with a flint, so there appears to be evidence for early-Saxon occupation, though it is always difficult to date objects to the fifth century. It is paradoxical that the two huts were built in the sunken road, demonstrating not only possible continuity of occupation but also the obstruction of the road

56 *Romano-British grain-drying oven in Toft 17 from the south, showing the first simple T-shaped period.*

to vehicular traffic, restricting it to a simple path between the huts.

Late-Saxon pottery was found but no contemporary structures. The date of the origin of the north manor house has not been established, but any Saxon high-status site will presumably be under the medieval earthworks. Although the sequence is not complete, the coincidence of a major Iron-Age site underneath the north manor house, with traces of Roman and Saxon occupation as well, does indicate that there might have been continued use of this area as a high-status complex over a period of some 1,500 years. From the medieval period a thirteenth-century grain-drying kiln (**35**) was found, showing that this was a grain preparation area separated off from the grain storage area with its barn to the west (**8**).

In Toft 17 a major medieval structure was found terraced into the boundary between the toft and croft, together with a later substantial outbuilding with chalk foundations, complementing the similar evidence from Toft 10 (p. 76). Neither of these buildings was visible on the surface so, like the building assumed to be

57 *View from the north of the Romano-British grain-drying oven in Toft 17 showing the later more complicated tuning-fork type plan, its front built up with the large dressed blocks of masonry taken from some major Roman building.*

a barn in the north of Area 6, they do not seem to have survived till the end of the fifteenth century.

The completion of Toft 10

When Area 10 was first excavated only the eastern half of the toft was investigated, since the building complex spread over the whole frontage, but no structures were found to the west of the area excavated. A reconsideration of the solar block of the twelfth-century manor house led to the realization that a timber hall may have lain south of the stone block (**97**). The south-west part of the site had originally not been excavated as it was much disturbed by medieval quarries and had also been used in the 1950s for the main spoil dump.

A 33-ft (10-m) square was therefore dug in 1977 to try to find the hall. Quarries, however, had disturbed all the evidence. Nevertheless, important (and unexpected) discoveries were made. On Area 10 itself only a few sherds of Saxon pottery were found in the 1950s, and it had been assumed that this was simply a scatter from manuring like the similar number of Roman sherds. In this new square many Saxon pottery sherds were found, the number increasing to the west. It was therefore clear that there was probably a major Saxon site in the western half of Tofts 9 and 10.

That area was therefore chosen for the second major excavation on the west plateau in the 1980s. The hope was to excavate a major Saxon site and at the same time complete the excavation of Toft 10. Beginning in 1980 a series of adjoining trenches was excavated, each usually taking two seasons to complete. Important evidence was recovered covering some 700–800 years of the village's history.

For the medieval period, two chalk-built outbuildings were found, associated with the late-medieval peasant houses. So, as in Toft 17, the peasant houses in Toft 10 had outbuildings at

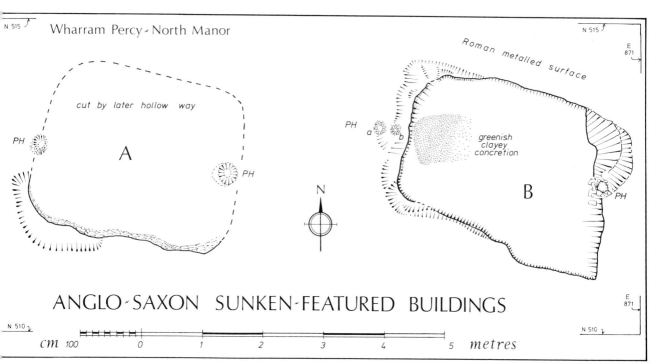

ANGLO-SAXON SUNKEN-FEATURED BUILDINGS

58 *Plans of the two Saxon* Grubenhäuser *cut into the main west-east road between Toft 17 and the North Manor. They have the characteristic rectangular sunken plan with a hole for a gable post at each end to hold up the roof.*

the back end of the toft and did not stand in isolation. Again these outbuilding were not visible on the surface, so they may have belonged to one of the earlier periods, when 9 and 10 were two different tofts, rather than the latest period, when there seem to have been only a peasant house and a barn in the eastern part of the toft.

The twelfth-century manor house, with its possible timber hall, had appeared to be the only manorial building, but the excavation of the western part of the toft also produced important new evidence for associated structures. A deep pit, 13 ft (4 m) wide at the top and 8 ft (2.5 m) deep, was found, interpreted as a cold store for food. Comparable examples are known, for example at Anlaby near Hull. It would have been the medieval equivalent of the seventeenth-century cold cellar at the post-medieval parsonage (p. 105) or the country house ice house before the invention of the refrigerator.

Nearby was a circular gully, enclosing a dry area that may have been a rick stand for hay or some other crop. Two cesspits were also found, probably the manorial latrines. No garderobe pit found was attached to the solar block itself, and the twelfth-century lord seems to have had a 100-ft (30-m) walk to his lavatory. These features have been added to the reconstruction in colour plates **9** and **13** in order to put the main buildings in context.

It was the Saxon levels underneath that provided the most important evidence. Some of the Saxon pottery in the first excavated square came from a deep spread of black earth full of pottery and bone. The sherds were unabraded, which has two important implications. Firstly, the rubbish was never cleared and spread on the fields as manure, unlike the Roman and medieval rubbish. Secondly the black earth had not been ploughed or dug over during medieval times. This suggests that at least this part of the back of the toft was not cultivated or churned up by animals. It may therefore have been either grass for grazing or an orchard.

Beneath, and preserved by the midden, were undisturbed Saxon features, most notably spreads of rubbish. The first four seasons' work on 2,100 sq ft (200 sq m), produced over 1,000 fragments of middle-Saxon pottery and many thousand bones, as well as the remains of a smith's workshop containing large quantities of slag. A series of post-holes suggests the presence of timber buildings, but so far their

77

size and nature remain unknown. The final two seasons of work in 1989 and 1990 are seeing the whole area of post-holes uncovered. In July 1989 the evidence seemed to suggest two successive buildings on different alignments.

The topsoil at Wharram is very variable, comprising chalk with clay pockets. It is of considerable interest that the Saxon people seem to have been aware of this, as they dumped their rubbish on the clay area and built their structures on the relatively well-drained solid chalk. The pottery and other finds from the western part of Toft 10 have not yet been processed, but the general impression is that the main bulk is from the middle of the seventh through the eighth and into the ninth centuries. The earliest find is a coin, a *sceat* of the first quarter of the eighth century, which fits in well with a radiocarbon date of AD 720 $\pm$ 80 from charcoal associated with the smithy. There is also some late-Saxon pottery, suggesting occupation into the Scandinavian period in the tenth century. This is confirmed by the discovery of a bronze fitting from a small strap, decorated with interlace patterns in the Borre style, datable to about 900 (**colour plate 5**) which although Scandinavian in origin was probably made in York. There is no evidence in Toft 10 for any occupation before the seventh century.

The most impressive earthwork at Wharram Percy is a bank on the plateau, separating the tofts of the west Row from their crofts. It stretches for 1,200 ft (380 m) from Drue Dale to the major east-west sunken road, which separates the peasant houses of the west Row from the north manor. The bank's size – it stands nearly 8 ft (2.5 m) high in places – as well as its apparent mutilation along parts of its length by medieval peasants suggested that it might be a prehistoric lynchet bank, formed by many years of ploughing, or one of the area's many Bronze-Age ranch boundaries (p. 91).

It seemed most unlikely that when the village was planned such a massive earthwork would be created simply to divide crofts from tofts. An earlier 5-ft (1.5-m) wide trench in toft 13 gave inconclusive results, so two 16-ft (5-m) sections were dug in the 1980s through this feature in Tofts 9 and 10. Although, typically, one area was almost entirely destroyed by a medieval building cut into the bank, there was sufficient evidence to show that the lynchet was post-Saxon at this point as the middle-Saxon features continued underneath it and reappeared to the west, though there was a Saxon ditch on the same line. It now seems likely that the bank was constructed in the twelfth century, and this in turn may suggest that the planning of the village dates to this time rather than the tenth century as had previously been thought (p. 84).

The problem still arises as to why the bank was so large. It seems to have been constructed of almost pure soil, which is why it had been thought to be a lynchet. If the soil came from turf, the areas of the tofts may have been deturfed and the turf built up to form a sod wall division between the tofts and crofts. If so, it is surprising that such good soil was not put on the fields, though turf walls are a feature of the Wolds. A further implication might be that the tofts and crofts were laid out at different times.

Further boundaries

The six areas excavated outside the main boundaries of the village further complicated the picture. At the bottom of Drue Dale water-logged natural deposits were found with no occupation, as might be expected in a wet site. A supposed post-medieval quarry at the south end of the west plateau, thought to be just outside Toft 4, was found in fact to be a late-Iron-Age or Roman quarry, utilized in the Saxon period and then included in Toft 4 in the medieval period, bounded by a stone wall. After the desertion of the village this wall was utilized to form one side of an aisled structure that may have been connected with the 250 years of sheep farming.

This excavation also showed that the present road here was post-medieval and not medieval. Similarly one of the two sunken roads coming up from near the cottages continuing west, cutting through the lynchet and obliquely across the medieval crofts, is now more likely to be later than the village, even though it does seem to head for one of the five Roman farms.

This Romano-British farm was at the back of what was later to be Croft 8. A complex sequence was found, with Saxon occupation extending into the twelfth century. It looks as though the area of the Roman farm was still occupied when the village was laid out, producing the kink in the west village boundary that was previously unexplained (**2**). Further evidence for this farmstead and its outer enclosures was found at the back of the later Croft 6.

To the north-east of the village, two areas were excavated outside the north boundary bank into which the eighth-century *Grubenhaus* (p. 68) was built. For the first time two 30-ft (9.1-m) squares were devoid of occupation, though one revealed stone stripes, formed under periglacial conditions at the end of the ice age. This is important as it does suggest that the northern village boundary might well also be the northern boundary of the area of prehistoric and Roman-British settlement and that the *Grubenhaus* was set into this outer boundary and was not in the centre of a Saxon settlement area. *Grubenhaüser* at the outer limits of settlements, along boundary banks, are a common feature, for example at Mucking in Essex.

So far this book has followed the progress of the excavation step by step. Each step was an attempt to answer its own particular question, the order of which was not necessarily logical. It is now time to present the reader with conclusions related to the whole plan of the village at different periods.

The village plan

When Beresford walked across the earthworks in June 1948 it seemed natural to assume that what he was looking at were the earthworks covering the ruined foundations of medieval peasant houses set in their enclosures, and that this was basically the village as laid out by the Anglo-Saxon invaders and settlers in the sixth century AD. A regular layout around a central green was in the 1950s regarded as one of the classic village types. Since then views on the development of villages and settlement generally have changed fundamentally. Wharram and other sites have shown that the situation was much more complex.

It has been one of the main strengths of the Wharram Research Project that the results have been assessed at the end of each three-week season so that new questions may be asked the next year. So, as the work has progressed, the research has developed with changing academic views. It is interesting to reflect what would have been the result if adequate funds had been available in 1953 for three years continuous excavation, which is about the actual time spent excavating over the last 40 years. It is likely that similar aspects of the village would have been examined, and

that the earlier features would have been discovered, but, with the then current ideas that villages had always comprised compact groups of houses since Saxon times, interpretation would have been very difficult. It is not much easier now, and the whole process is still imperfectly understood, but it is possible to draw general conclusions based on parallels with the considerable work done elsewhere in Britain and on the Continent on the medieval landscape.

If the basic layout of the village earthworks (2) is taken as the point from which the development can be traced both backwards and forwards, then it is immediately clear that the village was deliberately planned at some point in time. Its regularity shows that it did not grow haphazardly, as some villages seem to have done where there is an irregular plan. What could not be appreciated in 1948 was the extent to which the village earthworks had changed, not only during the medieval period but more remarkably, and only recently recognized, in the 500 years since the village was abandoned, a period in which it had been assumed that the site lay undisturbed both during its use as a sheep walk for 300 years and under the Improving Farm regime of the last 200 years.

It had generally been recognized that there were two parallel Rows of tofts and crofts and that, as they were not all filled with earthworks of ruined buildings, the numbers of occupied houses had gradually reduced, as the documents showed for the later medieval period, many perhaps before peasant houses were built with stone foundations. There was a separate manorial enclosure to the north and religious enclosures, the water mill and the fishpond to the south. This interpretation had been worked out both by survey on the ground and from the original RAF vertical air photograph of 1946 (6) and the sequence of oblique air photographs taken by Cambridge from 1948 onwards. With the taking of winter photographs in low sun, often enhanced by snow cover (59), it was assumed that the full potential of interpreting the earthworks had been utilized.

In 1979, however, the Royal Commission on Historical Monuments took a remarkable series of colour air photographs (**colour plate 1**) that completely changed our understanding of the site. In these, the long 1,300-ft (400-m) Row of tofts and crofts running north-south on the plateau was well defined, but there was quite a new view of the terrace. On the ground only the three northern tofts and crofts were clear, with possible signs of a fourth. The 1979 photographs clearly show a series of parallel toft boundaries continuing between these and the cottages. Excavations in these tofts demonstrated that they were occupied in the twelfth and thirteenth centuries but went out of use in the fourteenth, when they were presumably turned over to grazing, and the boundaries and the remains of houses became blurred.

Further excavations to the north and south of the surviving cottages have shown evidence for medieval buildings under the later farms but not for toft boundaries. Nevertheless it is likely that the regular layout of tofts and crofts extended the full length of the terrace as far as the parsonage. If the parsonage, churchyard and pond enclosures are added, then there is a regular Row running north-south on the valley floor and terrace, parallel with that on the plateau.

59 1978 oblique Cambridge air photograph from the north taken in ideal snow conditions, which bring up well the individual peasant house earthworks and the North Manor in the foreground. In the background the last remains of ridge and furrow are visible on the unploughed edge of the dales.

Even more remarkable was the discovery on the 1979 air photographs that the eastern part of the north manorial enclosure was not the open area it seemed but had once contained six tofts and crofts. The tofts had been amalgamated into a courtyard farm while the croft boundaries had been partially levelled. At some point in time, therefore, a regular village had been laid out with two north-south Rows, separated by a wedge-shaped central green, with a head Row at the northern end comprising a manor house, tofts and crofts (**34**). In addition a basic module of 60-ft (18.3-m) wide tofts seems to have been laid out, each the width of two selions, which at Wharram are on average 30 ft (9.1 m) wide (**2**).

Two factors have disturbed this regularity: firstly, the division or amalgamation of tofts, which makes the surviving widths variable; secondly, the gaps created by the decline of the village from about 30 to 16 houses in the fourteenth and fifteenth centuries, as demonstrated by the documents. Two new tofts were laid out when the Area 10 manor house was abandoned, about the same time that the six eastern tofts in the north Row were destroyed to make way for the fourteenth-century park. So the changes show a more complex pattern than simple decline (**60**). Finally there seem to have been further major changes in the earthworks during the 500-year post-desertion use when new roads were worn through the earthworks, new structures built for the sheep and possibly other changes made that can be proved only by excavation.

Before suggestions are made for the date of this planned village it is necessary to look at the evidence for earlier occupation both on the terrace and the plateau. There are signs of Neolithic occupation nearby, but not, so far, in any of the areas excavated, though several tree holes demonstrate the initial forest clearance. A scatter of Bronze-Age finds in the north

60 (right) Plan of the late-medieval village in decay in the fifteenth century, its 30 houses reduced to 16, leaving gaps in the centre of the west and east rows. The tofts and crofts in the eastern half of the north row were abandoned in the early fourteenth century and partly replaced by two new tofts and crofts on the site of the Area 10 Manor House, which had been abandoned after 1254.

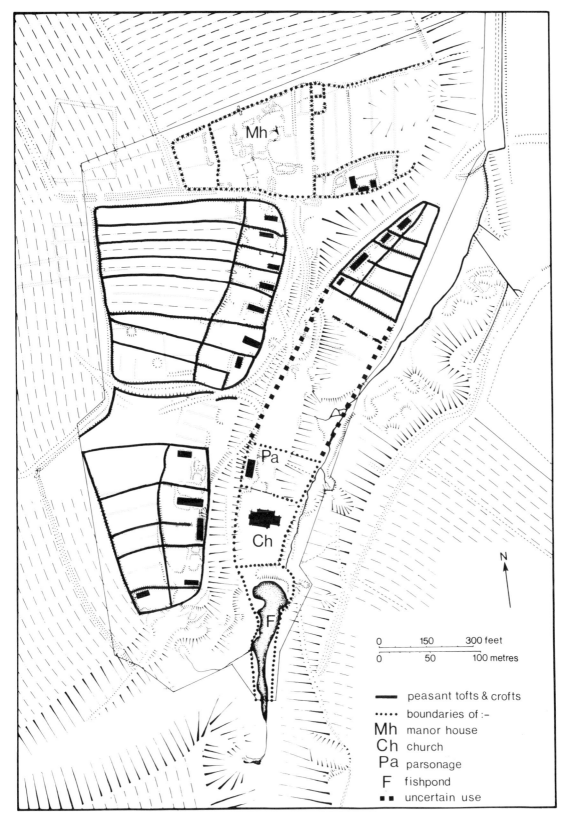

Mh

Pa

Ch

F

| 0 | 150 | 300 feet |
| 0 | 50 | 100 metres |

N

── peasant tofts & crofts
····· boundaries of :-
Mh manor house
Ch church
Pa parsonage
F fishpond
■■ uncertain use

81

manorial enclosure may suggest the date of the first occupation here, which might be linked with the use of the road by animals, giving access to drinking water in the valley from their grazing on the plateau at a time when the Wolds was being divided into ranching areas (p. 91). Unfortunately the lynchet can no longer be regarded as part of this system, although some of the medieval headlands may still be.

The first major evidence for intensive settlement comes from the early Iron Age, when farms were built on the area that was to become the north manorial enclosure and on the terrace north of the church. In the late Iron Age a regular series of enclosures was laid out to the north and south of the main east-west route up from the valley (53). There is likely to have been a similar ladder pattern of rectangular enclosures on the terrace, but this has been glimpsed only in the areas excavated.

In Roman times these farms continued to be occupied with only simple modifications of the general layout. The large amount of Romano-British occupation material found in the north-west enclosure and to the east along the northern ladder suggests that there were, in Roman times at least, two farms in this part of the site. Trial excavations in the space between suggest that the other enclosures formed paddocks or fields. Another Romano-British farm was built at the back of the later Areas 6–8, and occupation continued on the terrace with again possibly two foci, one under the site of the church and the other further north.

The general pattern therefore seems to suggest a steady expansion of settlement from two farms in the early Iron Age to at least five by the middle of the Roman period (53). As only 6 per cent of the area of the medieval village has been excavated there may well be more, but there seems to have been a series of farms, set about 650 ft (200 m) apart, forming a loose grouping rather than a village and presumably utilizing the preferred area of settlement provided by the plentiful water supply. Each farm could have used a different spring. The limitations of archaeological evidence make it impossible to determine whether these Romano-British farms were either independent or a grouping based on a possible Roman villa in the Wharram Percy area, for which there is some slight evidence (p. 71).

It is in the period between the end of Roman times, in the early fifth century, and the period of the formation of the medieval village that the story is still dark. It is uncertain how long the Romano-British farms continued once the Roman economy collapsed. It does, however, look as though at least one of the farms continued to flourish till quite late in view of the increase in capacity of the late-Roman grain-drying kiln.

The earliest evidence for the Saxon period comes with the sinking of the two sixth-century Grubenhäuser into the east-west main road out of the village (p. 71). There is a scatter of other early-Saxon pottery elsewhere but it is difficult to prove full continuity on the present evidence. In view of the fact that the north manor house was built on the site of a Romano-British farm and an earlier major Iron-Age site, it does seem likely that at least this enclosure remained occupied through the Saxon period but that other Romano-British farms may have been abandoned, suggesting a reduction in population but not complete abandonment. The south-west farm in Crofts 6–8 seems to have survived right up to the period of village formation, so that the village was laid out round it, preserving the odd kink in the western boundary of the medieval village.

The greatest surprise is that the terrace, which might be regarded as the best site, sheltered from the weather and near to water, seems to have been completely abandoned through both the early- and middle-Saxon periods – for 500 years perhaps, until the building of the church in the tenth century. Only a handful of Saxon pottery fragments has been found in the considerable area now excavated on the terrace, although there are animal bones datable to the middle-Saxon period as well as sceattas and stycas. Yet one must be cautious, since in Area 10 there was little such pottery in the eastern excavation but a large accumulation when the excavation was extended westward.

A major new middle-Saxon site appears to have been laid out in what was later to be the Area 10 manor, and seems to have been of high status in view of the early eighth-century sceat and the ironworking. The north manor area also seems to have risen to even higher status in the later eighth century from the evidence of another sceat, imported French Tating ware pottery and a good quality bone comb (61) in the northern Grubenhaus. In between Area 10 and the north manor, fragments of moulds for

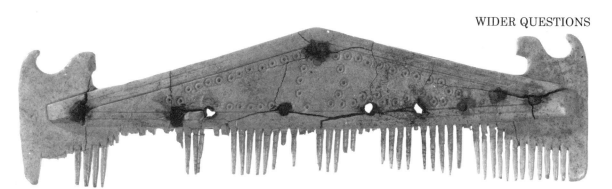

61 (above) *Eighth-century decorated bone comb found in the* Grubenhaus *near the north-east boundary of the village. Length 7.5 in. (19 cm).*

62 (below) *Fragment of Anglian cross arm decorated with simple carved interlace and datable to about AD 800. Maximum height 3.25 in. (8 cm).*

making copper-alloy objects were found in 1989 in the upper part of a Roman Ditch. The interlace decoration suggests an eighth-century date and, together with a crucible, suggest high status metal working. In addition the discovery of another *sceat*, together with a ninth-century strap end, part of an Anglian cross of *c.* AD 800 (**62**) and disturbed Saxon burials in Area 6, suggests that an Anglian church may not be far away from here.

Thus, by the seventh and eighth centuries, settlement at Wharram Percy seems to have revived to the extent that there were at least six main areas of settlement (**54**), a similar number to that in the Roman period, as well as evidence for some form of activity on the terrace. Five of these areas were of high status with evidence for metalworking, coins and imported pottery. The general picture is similar to that in the Roman period, with farms spaced irregularly in the landscape. The exact nature of the site is unclear but there is a distinct possibility that Wharram Percy may form one of the small family monastic sites that are known to have existed in the middle Saxon period. Another clue is that the cross fragment is not of local stone but carved from stone from the north of the Vale of Pickering where there are early monastic sites at Stonegrave and Lastingham.

From evidence elsewhere in England the change from scattered settlement to villages with compact groups of houses occurs during the late Saxon, Scandinavian or early medieval periods, that is in all periods between the ninth and the twelfth centuries. It is still unclear when it happened at Wharram and whether the planned village was laid out at the time when houses became grouped together, or whether the unsettled parts of the village gradually became filled in and the village was subsequently replanned.

There are two known historical occasions when major replanning could have occurred: either during the Scandinavian period in the tenth century, when there were clearly major tenurial changes – most settlements in the area were given Scandinavian names – and the pressure on population could have led to replanning, or after the dislocation caused by the harrying of the north after the Norman Conquest in the late eleventh century, when the village could have been replanned at the same time as the settlements were organized into parishes. The Scandinavian period still seems to be the most likely, since that was the period of the greatest possible dislocation, but if the lynchet is twelfth century this now suggests that the village may have been replanned at that time.

Planned villages occur so frequently on the Wolds that it would seem that whole areas of the landscape would have been involved in re-siting, possible after a Scandinavian invasion but less likely in the twelfth century when many different landowners would have been involved. One would also expect some documentary reflection of massive re-organization to have survived from the twelfth century, a period from which surviving charters and deeds are not uncommon, especially from monastic estates.

5

A further horizon

In the last decade of the excavations the research activity widened and deepened. On the one hand at the site itself many more specialist techniques were involved, not all of them strictly archaeological, while other investigations – historical as well as archaeological – spread beyond Wharram Percy.

The parishes survey

With only a fraction of the village site excavated, and that not devoid of ambiguities and perplexities, it might seem a rash strategy to embark on researches involving the four other townships of Wharram Percy parish and the adjoining single-township parish of Wharram le Street. Were not all these townships very similar to Wharram Percy: similar in area? similar in their natural resources of dale bottoms, dale sides and an expanse of Wolds plateaux? A mosaic of RAF vertical air photographs, constructed for display at an early stage in the excavations, had shown extensive ridge-and-furrow over all six townships, indicating that in the Middle Ages all had once had their open arable fields farmed in 'selions'. There was documentary evidence for *solskift* (p. 99) in all six, and everywhere the selions had been laid out with remarkable regularity. Today the outcome of their agricultural history is similar: large modern farms exploiting excellent arable land.

Similarly, the architectural history of the visible fabric of St Mary's, the parish church of Wharram le Street (the once 'Greater Wharram') did not seem very different from that at the other at Wharram Percy, once the 'Lesser Wharram'; well-preserved house earthworks at the deserted Towthorpe and others beyond the present limit of Wharram le Street suggested that here too were medieval long-houses with chalk foundations. Again, the houses in five of the seven villages bore signs of being deliberately laid out in two facing Rows, centred on a wide green. (At Burdale the village site was obscured by the construction of the railway station, sidings and embankment between 1847 and 1953; the site of Raisthorpe, indicated on the first Ordnance Survey plan as a small Row village, had been destroyed by more recent agricultural operations and tree planting.)

Had further excavations been the centre of ambition it would have been Towthorpe to which attention would have turned. A plan of the township dated 1772 had recently been acquired by the (then) East Riding Record Office whereon, although devoid of houses, the shapes of former tofts and crofts were clearly delineated and, as at Wharram Percy, the clarity of the house earthworks had attracted the attention of the first Ordnance surveyors.

In the event, the first extension of interest was into Wharram le Street. Prints of RAF vertical air photographs had been purchased as early as 1948, and in subsequent years and at different seasons the Cambridge University collection accumulated a series of Kenneth St Joseph's photographs while Tony Pacitto, a local archaeologist with a facility that enabled him to fly over the Wolds more frequently and at different seasons, would visit the excavation each year with an illuminating series of photographs of earthworks, crop marks and soil marks in the vicinity. The drought in the summer of 1976 was particularly productive of new data.

The photos demonstrated a complicated landscape of linear earthworks defining blocks of land, a network of trackways with ditches on either side, a series of ladder patterns comprising a linear alignment of enclosures, also defined by ditches and often fronting on to a trackway (**65**), and two Romano-British villa sites, one east of Wharram le Street and the other west of Wharram Grange Farm.

The air photography was followed up by an intensive programme of field-walking as the various fields became available between cropping. Most fields in the two parishes were

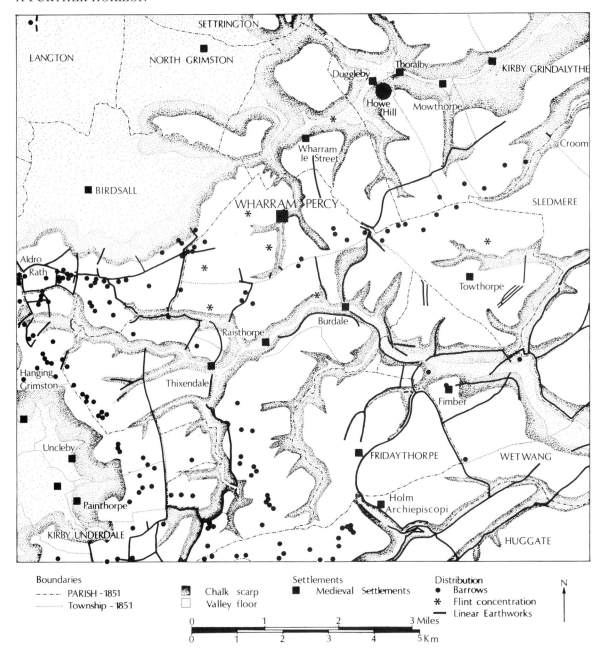

Boundaries
----- PARISH -1851
········· Township -1851

Chalk scarp
Valley floor

Settlements
■ Medieval Settlements

Distribution
● Barrows
✻ Flint concentration
— Linear Earthworks

N

0   1   2   3 Miles
0   1   2   3   4   5 Km

63 *Plan of features in the Wharram area on the north-west corner of the Wolds that are datable to the Neolithic and Bronze Ages. A very large Neolithic ceremonial enclosure was at Duggleby. Note the numbers of burial mounds and the Bronze Age and later linear earthworks which divided the countryside up into territories and large enclosures.*

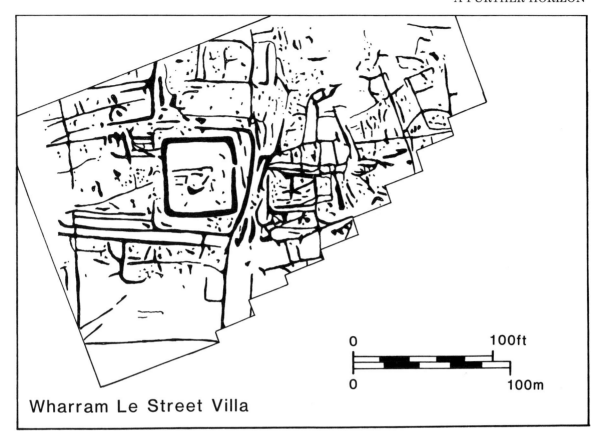

0   100ft

0   100m

Wharram Le Street Villa

64 *Geophysical survey of Roman villa at Wharram le Street, a little east of the medieval village. A regular series of rectangular enclosures can be seen with the main villa building in the central enclosure as well as a much more complex series of superimposed ditch system extending back to the Bronze Age. These are a large number of blobs which may represent storage or rubbish pits.*

walked randomly as a fairly rapid method of preliminary survey to locate sites not found by aerial photography and to pick up manuring spreads. These specific areas were then more extensively walked, often using crop rows, while occupation sites were gridded and field-walked in even greater detail. As most of the land is extensively cultivated, all the plateau tops have been investigated, the main gaps being the steep uncultivated hillsides and valley bottoms that remain under grass, as in the main Wharram valley.

Since 1979 the Ancient Monuments Laboratory have extended, to other sites in the parishes, their geophysical survey of the Guardianship area, which had yielded remarkably clear features under grass, especially the main east-west road to the north of the village with its small enclosures on either side and larger fields to the south. The two Roman villa surveys produced a remarkable amount of detail (**64**). In 1984 a survey was carried out along Birdsall Brow on four sample areas located by aerial photography, including sections of two farmstead sites and a ladder-pattern field system. The results have been most successful in pinpointing boundary ditches and other major features, but small details, like gulleys and post-holes, cannot always be found. There was another extensive pattern of settlement along the Gypsey Race (see below) between Wharram le Street and Duggleby (**65**).

This general survey work has been followed up by trial excavations across the two Roman villas and the Birdsall Brow Ladder enclosures.

87

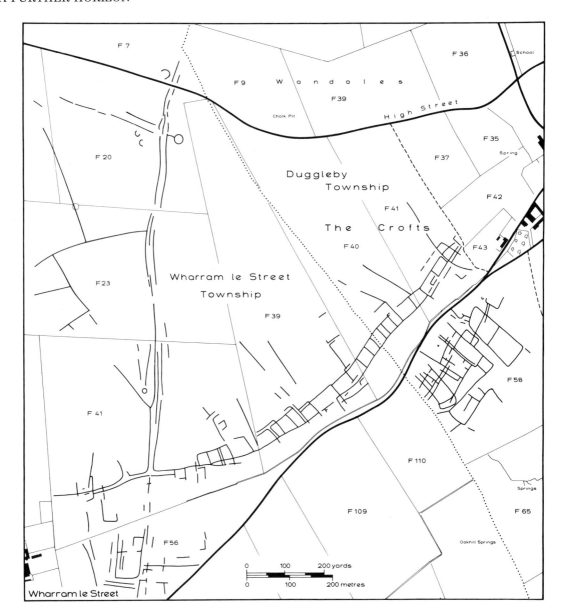

65a *Plan of the late-Iron-Age and Romano-British settlement along the north side of the Gypsey Race between Wharram le Street and Duggleby, plotted from the evidence of air photographs and comprising a series of rectangular ditched enclosures set in line forming a ladder pattern. A main north-south trackway, defined by ditches on either side runs down the plan while to the right is a more compact series of enclosures forming a farm with several periods of ditches.*

65b *1979 oblique air photograph of the Gypsey Race Iron-age settlement showing up as cropmarks. At the centre is the ladder pattern of enclosures and, across the middle, the ditched road. Compare with **65a**. The Wharram le Street Roman villa was in the triangular field on the right. The circular feature is the source of the Gypsey Race. Looking east.*

Surveys of the earthworks denoting settlement shrinkage at Wharram le Street have also been followed up by trial sections. As a result of over 15 years of this multidisciplinary work, a general picture has been built up of the development of the landscape of the two Wharram parishes.

Prehistoric and Roman settlement

Some of the earliest evidence for human activity in the Wharram area comes from late Mesolithic flints found around the source of the Gypsey Race, a stream that rises in Wharram le Street and then flows down the Great Wold Valley to the North Sea at Bridlington (1). These Mesolithic hunters presumably visited the Wolds seasonally after forest became established in the post-glacial period, Neolithic farmers were clearing areas after 3500 BC, and two phases of clearance, separated by a period of woodland regeneration, have been recognized by an examination of the fossil soils

89

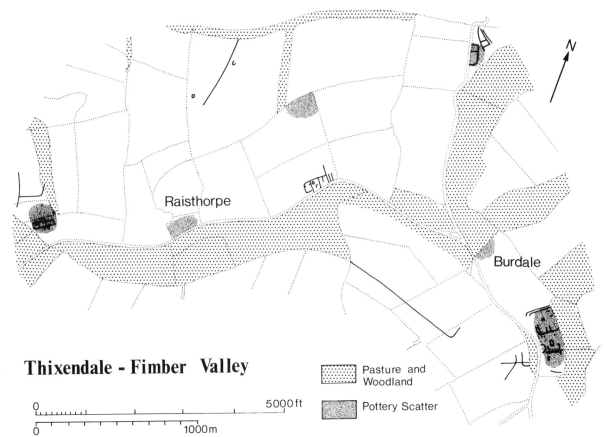

Thixendale - Fimber Valley

Pasture and Woodland

Pottery Scatter

Raisthorpe

Burdale

0   5000 ft

0   1000 m

66 *Plan of the settlements along the Thixendale–Fimber valley south of Wharram showing the deserted medieval villages of Raisthorpe and Burdale, which were on the sites of Iron Age and Romano-British farms, with other deserted Iron Age and Romano-British farms between. Thixendale lies just to the left and Fimber just to the right, showing the regular spacing of early settlements and then the abandonment of alternate sites when the medieval villages were formed and the outlying settlements concentrated.*

preserved beneath long barrow burial mounds excavated on the nearby Wolds.

Possible evidence for forest clearance at Wharram is provided by six imported Langdale stone axes from Cumbria which may have been used to cut down the primary wildwood. Treeholes, filled with brown forest soil, have been excavated. Possible occupation sites are suggested by scatters of Neolithic flints, including scrapers, knives and arrowheads, but the exact nature of the settlement is hard to determine on the High Wolds because of the erosion

of the thick brown forest soils which would have covered the area. There is good evidence for this erosion in the valley at Wharram Percy, with the thick deposits of hillwash caused by continued disturbance of the ground for arable cultivation in Neolithic and later times.

In the later Neolithic there appear to have been changes in the economy and ritual practices. Monuments of a new type appeared, the round barrow becoming the principal form of burial monument. There are many of these at Wharram, especially along the ridgeway (**63**); a large number were opened by Mortimer in the nineteenth century. The largest barrows in East Yorkshire are located along the Great Wold Valley: the most westerly of this series is Duggleby Howe, 124 ft (38 m) in diameter and standing 20 ft (6 m) high.

Only 1.5 miles (2 km) east of Wharram le Street and 2 miles (3.5 km) from Wharram Percy, the Howe stands at the centre of the crop-marks from a large Neolithic ceremonial monument detected from the air. This enclosure, with interrupted ditches, is 1,200 ft (370 m) in diameter and is one of the largest Neolithic monuments in the country. It was doubtless the main Neolithic centre for the western Wolds, as Rudston, with its ritual sites and the largest stone monolith in the country, appears to have been in the east. The Great Wold Valley with the Gypsey Race would have provided a major settlement corridor.

Extensive utilization of the Wolds in the Bronze Age is shown by the numerous round barrows, but the most significant feature is the series of linear earthworks that divide the

landscape into large enclosures (**63**). They are hard to date, but it is likely that the first examples are middle Bronze Age, becoming more complex in the Iron Age. Their existence presupposes full exploitation of the landscape, whether for grazing or arable, as there would otherwise have been no need for land allotment and division. The large number of flint scrapers, which would have been used for preparing animal skins, and the few blades, used for cutting cereals, may suggest a greater emphasis on grazing.

It was in the late Iron Age, however, that the landscape became fully settled. The large enclosures were subdivided with farmsteads situated at about 0.6-mile (1-km) intervals along the main valleys, joined by double-ditched track-

67 *Features in the Wharram area that are datable to the Iron-Age and Romano-British period.*

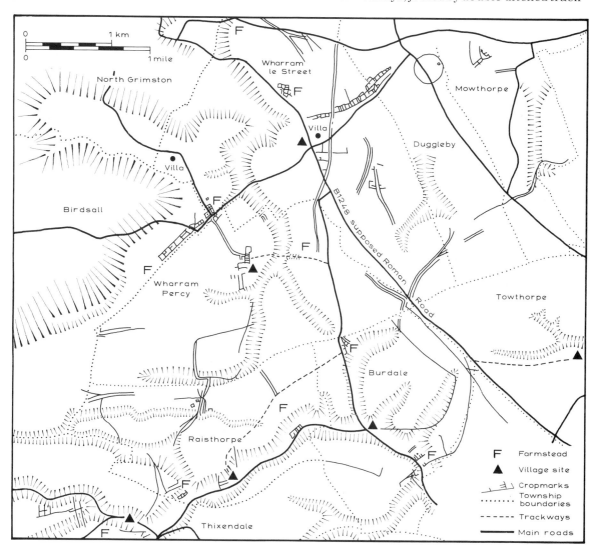

ways, and associated with ladder pattern enclosures (66). That this landscape is pre-Roman is most clearly demonstrated south of Wharram le Street, where the Roman road south from Malton cuts obliquely across this landscape in the same way as a modern railway or motorway cuts earlier field boundaries.

The excavations of the ladder patterns at Wharram Percy confirm a pre-Roman dating for these earthworks. There have been 31 sites including 11 farmsteads and four ladder patterns, identified in the Wharram parishes. As most of these have produced mainly Romano-British pottery from field-walking it is not possible to say which date from the Iron Age and which originated through a Roman expansion, but most are likely to be pre-Roman in origin. The main developments in the Roman period were the two villas of higher status, being either the centres of estates providing

68 *Raithorpe township showing the present farm on the site of the deserted medieval village and a Romano-British farm. The dots represent the findspots of Roman pottery fragments resulting from spreading manure on the fields. Assuming that the township is the same area as the Romano-British farm, then only the core area was manured. fx = modern field number.*

food for the population of Roman Malton or the country houses of Roman officials in the town (64).

The spacing of the settlements is generally about every half mile (1 km), especially along the Thixendale valley where there is a medieval village every 1 mile (1.6 km) and a Romano-British farm halfway between (66). Four of the six medieval villages have so far produced evidence for Roman or earlier settlements on the same site, and the others might produce material if they were more fully studied.

These settlements had manuring scatters associated with them but only over limited areas (68). It is hard to tell if these indicate the bounds of arable cultivation or whether such areas were just cultivated more intensively, as in the medieval period, with an infield/outfield system (p. 96). The ladder-pattern sites are particularly enigmatic since it is unclear whether these enclosures were arable fields with stock in the gaps between or whether the enclosures were for stock with arable fields of unknown extent between. The large areas of manuring round the farmstead sites strongly suggest the latter.

In the Saxon period the main evidence for settlement is on those sites that were to become

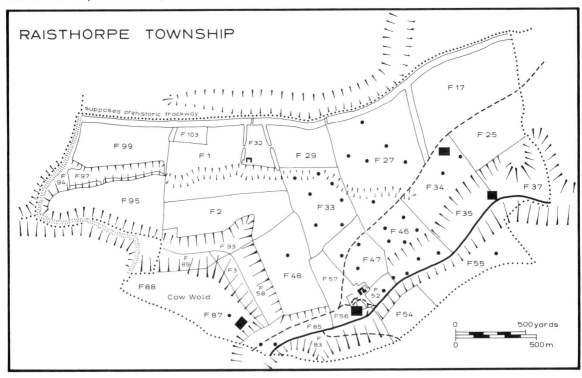

RAISTHORPE TOWNSHIP

supposed prehistoric trackway

F 17
F 25
F 99
F 103
F 32
F 1
F 29
F 27
F 97
F 94
F 34
F 37
F 95
F 33
F 35
F 2
F 46
F 93
F 47
F 55
F 89
F 3
F 48
F 57
F 88
F 58
F 52
Cow Wold
F 56
F 54
F 87
F 85
F 83

0   500 yards
0   500 m

villages with houses grouped together. There is also evidence for the Roman sites between the larger sites continuing into the Saxon period, but they were abandoned before medieval village formation. This is partly because Saxon rubbish does not seem to have been put on the fields in the same quantity as in Roman or medieval times (p. 96). It is only between Wharram Percy and Wharram Grange that

69 *An 1810 estate plan of Wharram-le-Street showing a regular layout on either side of the main north-south Roman road, with the church offset to the south-west, the whole village being enclosed by a regular boundary bank. The present village plan with gaps caused by shrinkage and the nineteenth- and twentieth-century houses built along the west-east road is very deceptive and obscures the medieval plan.*

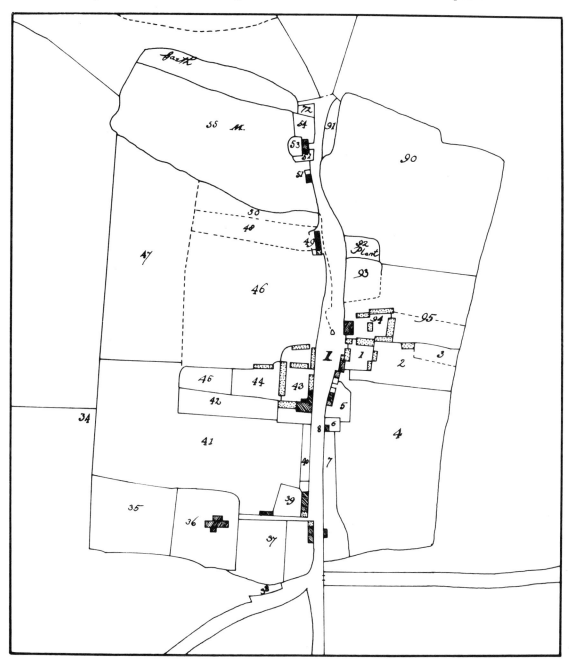

there are widespread scatters of Saxon pottery. These are not evenly spaced, as from manuring, but form clusters that may be the evidence for scattered farmsteads set in widely-spaced groups rather than at larger but more equal intervals as in the Roman period. These scatters are, however, very hard to interpret without a major excavation programme.

70 *Deserted medieval village of Raisthorpe: oblique air photograph from the east showing the earthworks of a regularly planned village with rectangular tofts and crofts on either side of the main road, taken in 1956 under grass. The site has now been ploughed up and over-planted (Crown copyright: MOD photograph).*

This leads forward to the problems of when the village was formed, but the recovery of evidence for this from the rest of the parishes will involve much further research. There is an almost complete lack of late-Saxon pottery on the fields between settlements, which is one of the reasons why it was thought that the compact grouping of houses to form villages took place in this section of the Wolds during the Scandinavian period in the tenth century. Although some archaeological evidence seems to suggest that the planned settlements were twelfth century (p. 78), it is possible that the scattered settlements became more concentrated as the Saxon period progressed, so that village formation happened gradually. Many of

the other villages in the area were planned as regular street villages. Wharram le Street is a very clear example (**69**), and trial excavations of the earthworks suggest that it was laid out in the twelfth century, as Wharram Percy may have to have been. Other local planned villages were Raisthorpe (**70**) and Thixendale (**72**).

71 *Reconstruction from air photographs and ground survey of the field system that once covered the whole area of Towthorpe township except the steep dale sides. Except for some small areas the whole system is laid out regularly in selions running north-south, up to 3300 ft (1000 m) in length and ignoring the lie of the land. The site of the deserted village and the two surviving farms lies in the centre.*

The open fields

Whatever the period of replanning, that was presumably also the time at which the open fields were organized. The evidence for the medieval field systems in the six Wharram townships has been surveyed. The reconstruction of the medieval open field system is based mainly on aerial photography. The selions often give rise to crop marks, and ridge and furrow remains visible under grass in the Wharram Percy Farm paddocks. The quality of the crop marks is partly due to the selions being preserved for centuries in the grass of the sheep walks, until the final ploughing up of the Wolds after the Second World War. The evidence on the ground was then examined, especially for headlands.

A remarkable regularity was found. The Wolds selions stretch for up to 3,200 ft (1,000 m) in the same direction, ignoring the general

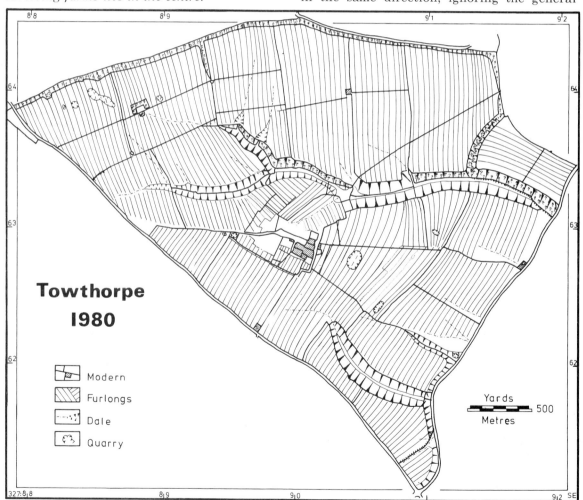

Towthorpe 1980

Modern
Furlongs
Dale
Quarry

Yards
500
Metres

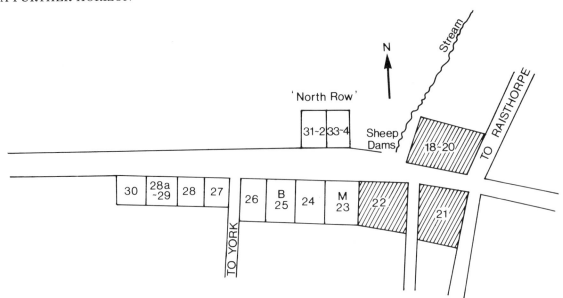

72 *The suspiciously regular elements in the Thixendale village plan are (i) bovate-holders occupied the group of four identical sized crofts on the west of the York Road and a second group of four with longer backsides to the east; two others faced them across the single village street, and were once known as 'North Row'; (ii) the three crofts at the east end of the village (shaded) are larger and irregular and their owners never possessed bovates in the open fields. Numbers relate to a plan and survey of 1793: M, the former manor house, and B, a former tithe barn.*

topography (**71**). With their coming, the Iron-Age landscape was completely changed, the scattered settlements being overlaid by the new field system and the winding tracks replaced by regular access headlands between the furlongs. The Wharram selions may have been laid out in long strips because of the light chalk soil, which enabled ploughing to be carried out easily. It is further likely that much of the ploughing was done by horses, rather than oxen, and that they would be able to plough for longer stretches without stopping (**28**). Certainly the large quantities of horse bones found at Wharram would support this (p. 44).

Since whole areas of the Wolds plateau were laid out with these regular strips, all the land except the steep hillsides and the bottoms of the dales, which presumably provided grazing and meadow, must have been cultivated. There was no land left for woodland, which must also have been in the valleys or on the slopes, as it

still is on the Wold scarp. The replanning, therefore, seems to have taken place at a period when population pressure necessitated the full exploitation of the Wolds. This would be more likely to have been reached in the twelfth century than in Scandinavian times.

The universality of the selions does not necessarily mean that the whole parish was simultaneously ploughed. Field-walking has shown that only certain areas near to the villages were manured, suggesting an intensively cultivated infield with a less used outfield. It is striking that not only is this similar to the Roman usage (p. 92) but also many of the areas are the same, as if certain core land was kept in better shape. This makes more likely a continuity at the most important Roman settlements that became villages. The Romano-British estates, which may indeed have been laid out in the Iron Age, may thus have formed the basis of the later townships, providing continuity of boundaries as well. Certainly the present boundaries existed in the period when the open fields were laid out as there is discontinuity of the selions at the township boundaries.

Open-field agriculture, a relatively modern term, takes its name from the absence of dividing hedge, walls and fences within the cultivated area, and that in turn was associated with access to common rights of grazing, which

1 Air photograph of the medieval village earthworks: oblique view from north-east showing the main north-south road through the site with rectangular tofts, crofts and house earthworks on either side.

2 Reconstruction drawing of the parish church of St Martin as it may have looked in the late twelfth century (Period V) with the semicircular apse at the east end and the addition of the south aisle. The possible vicarage is shown south of the church; in the foreground is the small pond and horizontal-wheel watermill for grinding corn. On the plateau behind are the peasant houses to the left and the twelfth-century manor house to the right.

3 View from the south-west showing on the left the marked out peasant houses in Area 6, the red-tiled-roof cottages and, further to the right, the vicarages in the process of excavation, the ruined church and graveyard and the reconstructed medieval fishpond.

4 General view from the east of the fully-excavated nave in 1974 showing in the foreground the foundations of the late-Saxon stone church and the extensive disturbance from the digging of the burials.

5 Borre-style bronze fitting decorated with interlace ornament, *c.* AD 900; length 1.3 in (3.5 cm).

6 A twelfth-century faced stone with characteristic diagonal tooling, marked out for the game of Nine Men's Morris. This was found in the mill area and was either from the miller's house or debris from a rebuild of the church.

7 Three grave slabs of late-Saxon lords found in the south-east angle of the nave and the chancel in 1973. That in front has a simple cross, and the two behind —the left that of a child—have simple ribs. All had head and footstones which were cut off at ground level when the Norman church was built.

8 Close up of the burial of a priest, found in the north-east chapel in 1963, with lead copies of the chalice and paten used for celebrating Mass.

9 Reconstruction drawing of the Area 10 manor house from the south-east showing the excavated solar block to the right and the supposed timber-built hall in the centre. Associated structures behind include a hayrick stand and a lavatory.

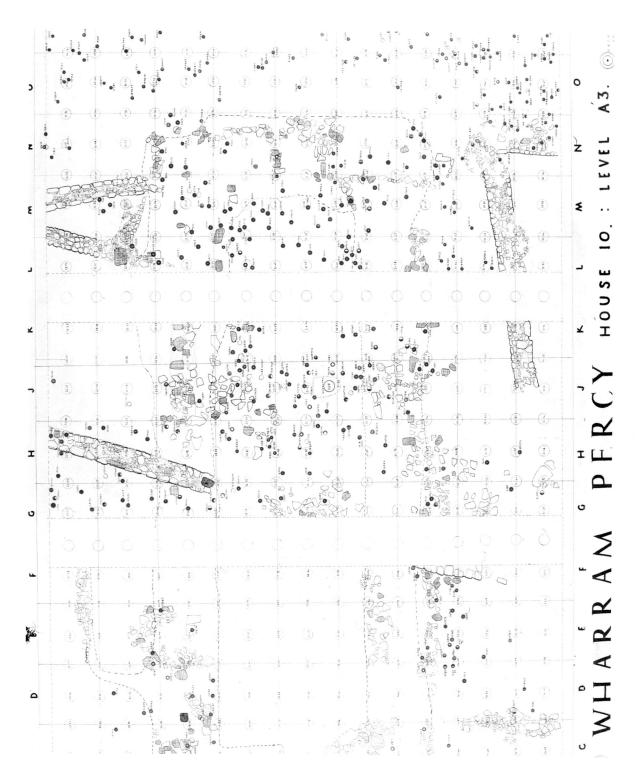

WHARRAM PERCY · HOUSE 10. : LEVEL A3.

10 General view of the Area 10 manor house undercroft in process of excavation in
1957. Maurice Beresford is seen top left and John Hurst top centre.

11 Area 6: volunteers trowelling the central portion of the excavated area in 1962.

12 A fair copy of the 1954 field drawings of Level A3 showing the small lengths of
wall found and the various finds plotted.

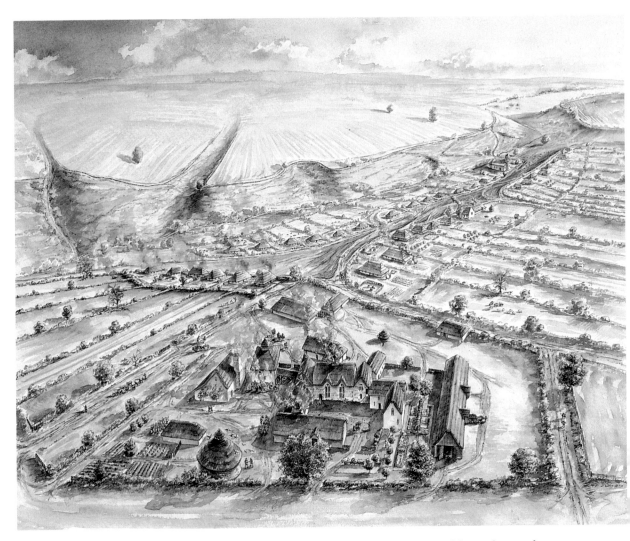

13 Reconstruction drawing of how the village might have looked from the north with the north manor house in the foreground, the three Rows of peasant houses, tofts and crofts with a central wedge-shaped green. The Area 10 manor house and church are seen towards the back right and the ridge and furrow of the open fields beyond.

existed when a portion of the land was left fallow for recuperation, and to the selions (see below). In the absence of any field divisions in the modern sense, the term 'Field' was reserved for those very large subdivisions of the arable area by which the annual rotation of fallow was organized.

The multiplicity of selions within open fields can best be appreciated where there survives a large-scale plan surveyed before enclosure, such as those from such local villages as Kilham or Skirpenbeck. There is none surviving for any of the six Wharram townships. Post-enclosure plans for Thixendale and Towthorpe show the position of the great Fields but not the furlongs and selions. Thus there is no cartographic evidence to set alongside the reconstructions made by Hall (above, p. 71) from air photographic and field-walking evidence. The only pre-enclosure written survey (or 'field-book') covering the whole of a Wharram township is that for Thixendale drawn up in 1793, but its smallest unit was the flatt or furlong, and it did not particularize each selion's position. A valuable insight into the topography of local open-field agriculture is however afforded by descriptions of small holdings of land in Wharram le Street and Raisthorpe in the great field-book of the Dacre estates in 1563, which is preserved at Castle Howard.

The Wharram le Street holding was particularized in that survey as lying within five separate Fields (South, Haver, West, Oxcroft and North) and that at Raisthorpe within three (East, South and West). The survey had further sub-headings: the selions at Raisthorpe were listed under headings that named 15 separate 'Furlongs' with names like 'White Hill' and 'Kirk Holme' and those of the larger holding at Wharram le Street lay within 26 named Furlongs, including 'the Furlong between the Grange and the Town' and 'Mill Hedge Furlong'. A Furlong was a block of selions literally a furrow-long rather than a modern unit of length, 220 yd (200 m). Within each Furlong the plough teams had always laid out the long narrow selions in the same direction, but from Furlong to Furlong that direction varied, as Figure **71** shows. Thus only seven of the 58 selions in the Wharram le Street holding were described in 1563 as running east-west, the remainder being north-south, and only eight of the 30 surveyed in Raisthorpe ran east-west.

There is a single piece of earlier evidence from Wharram Percy township: when dower land was allocated out of the manorial demesne in 1368 all the selions in one named Furlong, '*Medelgate*' (Middlegate), ran north-south.

The widths of the selion are not stated in any document but they must have varied since some were described in the Dacre survey as 'a brod lond' (containing $1-1\frac{1}{2}$ acres (0.4–0.6 ha)) and others as 'a narrow lond' ($\frac{1}{8}-\frac{1}{4}$ acres (0.05–0.1 ha)). When the small cluster of undisturbed ridge-and-furrow in paddocks near Wharram Percy Farm was recently measured the former selions had an average width of 31 ft (9.4 m).

The ancient local name for a unit agricultural holding was 'oxgang', often interchanged with 'bovate'. In a township each oxgang holder would have roughly the same area of arable land (in selions) together with an allocation of meadow land, but the area of an oxgang varied between townships. The Dacre bovates at Wharram le Street had $22\frac{1}{2}$ acres (9.1 ha), and those at Raisthorpe $17\frac{1}{4}$ acres (7 ha). In 1440 Haltemprice Priory, then the owners of the living at Wharram Percy, reduced the vicar's stipend but compensated him with a house and two oxgangs of land from an endowment of manorial land that had been presented to them a century earlier when there had been at least 29 other bovates in the lord's demesne and 41 held by unfree (villein) tenants. As late as 1743 the glebe terrier was continuing to record the two bovates of 1440 and the names of the Furlongs where their component selions had lain.

Not all the land in the Wharram townships was arable: the $35\frac{1}{2}$-acre (14.4-ha) holding in the open fields of Wharram le Street that was surveyed in 1563 had another $7\frac{1}{2}$ acres (3 ha) for hay ground, lying in 14 places in the village's three pieces of meadow. After harvest and haymaking there were common rights of grazing that were also linked to the number of bovates held. In 1563 Lawrence Cooper, the Dacre tenant at Raisthorpe

> may kepe by force of his Tenement [of two oxgangs] before the comon neyt [ox and bullock] herd[sman] iii [3] kien [kine] and may putt into the Oxe pasteer [pasture] iii plough cattall. An may also kepe xx [20] shepe for every oxgang.

So long as open field husbandry continued, the term *oxgang* was employed. Thus when virtually all the villagers' holdings at Thixen-

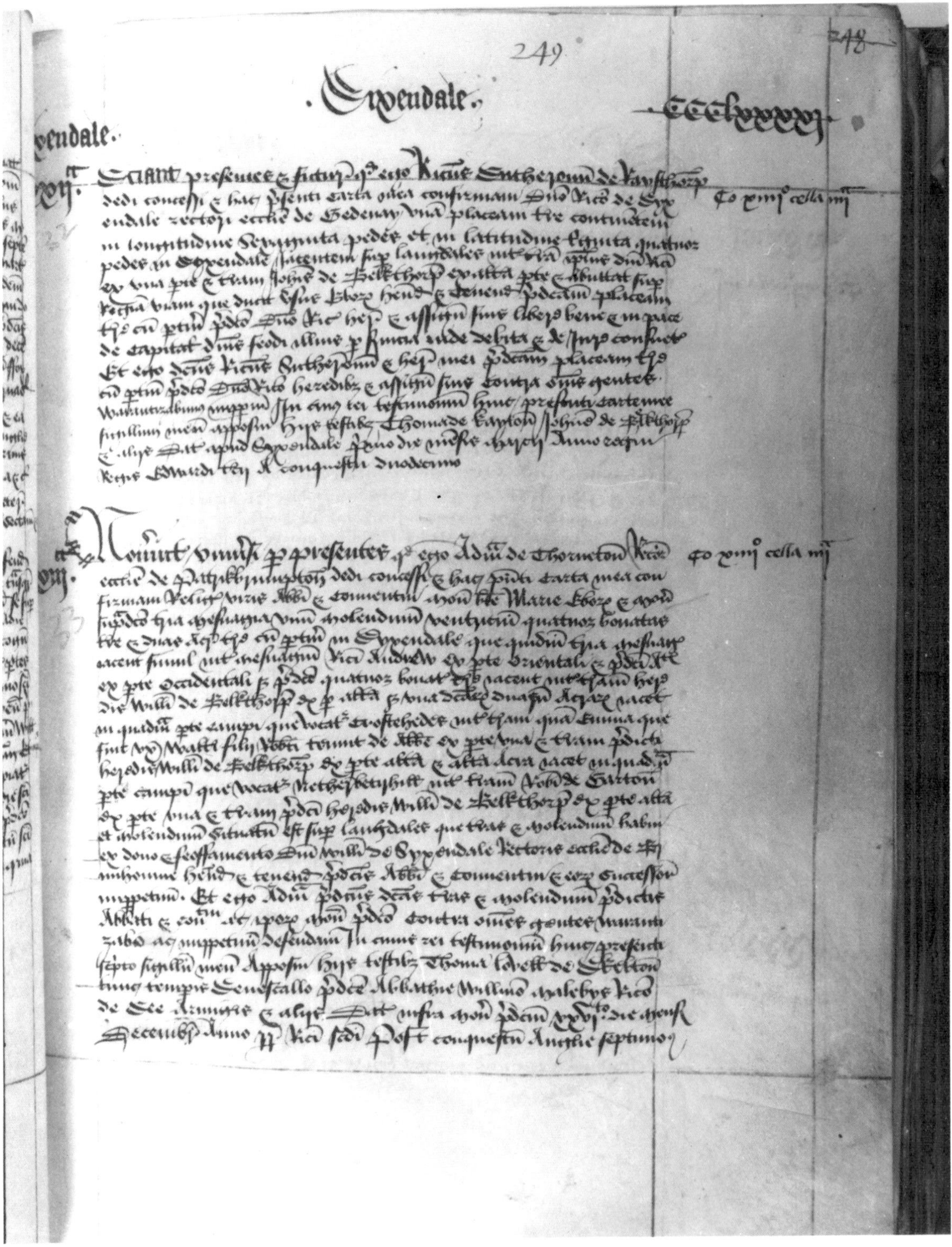

249

Expendale

Expendale.

[The page contains two medieval Latin charter entries written in a cursive manuscript hand, largely illegible.]

73 *St Mary's Abbey land in Thixendale. A folio, originally numbered ccclxxxxi (391), from the cartulary of St Mary's Abbey, York. The lower paragraph records a grant to the abbey by Adam de Thornton, rector of Patrick Brompton, of [line 4] three messuages, a windmill, four bovates and two acres of land in* Syxendale. *Locations are given: the messuages are adjacent and have Richard Andrew's messuage on their east, and another of the Abbey's on the west; the windmill [line 14] is situated above* Langdales. *The grant was made [final line] on 26 December on the 7th year of Richard II's reign (1383). The upper paragraph records an earlier grant made of the site for the windmill above* Langdales *from Richard Sutherom de Raisthorpe to Richard de Thixendale, rector of Gedney, Lincs. The piece of land measured [line 4] 60 feet [18 m] by 34 feet [10.2 m], the latter perhaps a selion's width. It conveniently abutted on the King's highway to York. The grant was made [final line] on 1 March in the 12th year of Edward III (1338).*

dale were conveyed to Sykes of Sledmere, between 1786 and 1798, the lawyers' conveyances were still describing them as so many oxgangs, more than 100 in all. It is possible from the exceptionally long run of deeds in the Sykes archive to determine which of these had been part of monastic endowments before the Dissolution: 34 belonged to Kirkham compared with the lord of the manor's 26. Similarly at Wharram le Street the number of oxgangs once belonging to Meaux Abbey and Nostell Priory is known, here because lawsuits extending from 1595 to 1598 produced sworn statements from old men of the village who recalled how many oxgangs had been monastic land before 1536, making their present owners able to claim exemption from tithe. Of the 100 oxgangs, 40 had belonged to the Cistercian abbey of Meaux, which had a grange in the western part of the township where the name of the present Wharram Grange farm perpetuates its memory.

The substantial proportion of monastic land in these two villages may help to explain why no single landowner had been able to acquire all the holdings and go in for grazing. At neither Burdale nor Wharram Percy, the earliest to be depopulated, was there monastic holdings of any size: in the latter the four bovates were given to Haltemprice, and at Burdale a small holding was given to St Mary's, York.

Monasteries commonly preserved written evi-

dences of their endowments in volumes known as cartularies, and of those religious houses with property in the Wharram parishes such volumes survive (in whole or part) from the monastic houses at Kirkham, St Mary's York, Old Malton, Meaux and Nostell. The grants setting out these endowments often embody phrases locating tofts and crofts in the village streets and naming highways leading to the wider world.

It is from a cartulary, for example, that the existence is known of medieval windmills in the fields of the comparatively waterless Thixendale, but the most important information from cartularies about the ancient topography concerns *solskift* (**74**), a system that presupposes an early, deliberate and ordered laying out of selions in a way that matches the other evidence (p. 74) for an ordered regularity of tofts and crofts within the villages (**72**). Evidence for *solskift* can be found for all six Wharram townships.

Solskift (from the Scandinavian 'sun share') distributed the selions of the bovate holders in such a way that within every Furlong their selions lay in the same order: there is some evidence that this order was also that of the houses along the village street, counting clockwise from east to west (hence the 'sun'). Thus the selions in two bovates at Raisthorpe given to the vicar of Wharram Percy in 1385 lay *juxta*

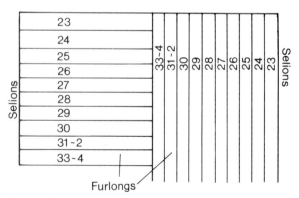

74 *Schematic arrangement of selions in solskift. There is much documentary evidence for a regular distribution of ownership for the selions throughout the 12 furlongs of the open fields. If it followed solskift, then the bovate holders in Thixendale would have held their selions in the clockwise order of the crofts, east to west: 23, 24, 25, 26, 27, 28, 29, 30, 31 and 33, as in the diagram and Figure 72.*

solem (next to the sun) in the Furlongs of each Field. The Kirkham Priory selions in Thixendale were *propinquiores sole* (nearest to the sun), and the same term appears among the Burdale lands in the cartulary of St Mary's Abbey, York (**73**). This abbey was given four bovates at Thixendale in 1383, which were 'lying always between the lands of the heirs of William de Barkthorpe', and in the village street each of the bovate-holder's houses lay between houses belonging to the same William's heirs.

6

The site after desertion

Archaeological evidence apart, there can be no doubt that as a village community Wharram Percy had ceased to exist by the early sixteenth century. The village was certainly shrinking in size in the previous century although still having at least 16 households in 1458. In the absence of manorial records from the next half century it will always be uncertain whether agricultural depression then continued to reduce the number of occupiers or whether the landlord was under the same temptation as those landlords in the Midlands who were pillored for reducing employment by deliberately turning arable into sheep pasture. Certainly with the expansion of woollen clothmaking in the Pennine villages to the west there would have been every incentive to increase the number of fleeces, and the fact that prosecutions in 1517 were alleging recent evictions, albeit only of four households, suggests that the absentee landlord had succumbed to temptation.

Without villagers and in single ownership the pastures were available for letting, although until the late sixteenth century the identity of the tenants is obscure. Some flock masters certainly lived in other villages and brought in their sheep, and for a while there was a non-resident vicar living in Wharram le Street who let the vicarage house to a farmer.

With a distant landlord there was no one to occupy the manor house. Thus the earthworks on the main village site do not include a post-medieval manor house and, since there are also none that would be appropriate to a post-medieval farmstead, the sheepmasters or their shepherds must have lived elsewhere. The most likely site is on one of the medieval house sites near the vicarage (below, p. 112).

The sixth of successive Sir William Hiltons sold the manor in 1573 to Matthew Hutton, Dean and later Archbishop of York, whose nephew then sold it in 1636 to Sir John Buck of Filey. There are no estate records surviving for this period, but the names of the tenant farmers are known intermittently, principally from taxation records and the parish register. The tone of a few leases from this period do suggest that, as elsewhere in England, economic circumstances no longer gave unrestrained encouragement to pastoral husbandry and some ground was returned to arable (below, p. 116. Perhaps it was at this stage that a rather more substantial house was built on the site next to the vicarage. Early-seventeenth-century taxation assessments, which touched only men of some substance, have several names under the heading Wharram le Street and one under Wharram Percy. John Richardson, an early-seventeenth-century tenant at Wharram Percy, was wealthy enough to figure among those forced to pay Charles I to avoid the burdens of compulsory knighthood. Amongst the 1989 finds was a fragment from a rare type of Rhenish stoneware jug, datable to the early seventeenth century, which is likely to have belonged to John Richardson.

In 1670–4 the collectors of the Hearth Tax recorded only two houses at Wharram Percy: the vicarage with three hearths and another two-hearth dwelling (**75a** and **b**) of which the foundations were identified during the 1989 season of excavations. Thus from the early sixteenth century onwards the centre of occupation, for the first time in 2,000 years, had moved down from the plateau, and henceforward 'Wharram Percy' would be the small group of buildings in the valley: the church, the vicarage and the farmstead.

The parsonages
The survival of the vicarage was due to the continued use of the church by inhabitants of the other townships in the parish, although after the depopulation of Towthorpe and Raisthorpe in the late seventeenth century (below, p. 108) it was effectively for the use of Thixendale villagers alone, however inconveniently it

75a & b *The two Wharrams in the Hearth Tax, 1674. At* Wharam P[er]seye *there were only two houses, the farm (Mr Bacon) with 3 hearths and the vicarage (Mr Luckock) with two. This extract continues with* Wharam in ye Strett *where there were 12 houses (27 hearths): there were also 13 relieved of payment through poverty. At Towthorpe (right) there are still 13 houses.*

was placed for them. In 1743 the vicar, William Mills, reported to the archbishop that 'all my Parishioners except one Family live two Miles from the Parish Church'.

There had been abortive moves to remove the anomaly in 1650 by amalgamating the livings of the two Wharrams and allocating the remote townships to other parishes, but although an amalgamation was eventually achieved in 1834 the townships of Wharram Percy remained in the parish. A proposal that had been made in 1829 to move the church fabric to Thixendale was also abortive, and, although some relief was afforded in 1854 by licensing a schoolroom for public worship, the village – now with over 30 houses – did not have its own church until one was provided in 1870 at the gift of Sir Tatton Sykes, on whose estate Thixendale then lay.

Vicars were certainly resident at Wharram Percy until the mid eighteenth century but thereafter they often held other adjoining livings in plurality and resided elsewhere, usually at North Grimston since the Wharram le Street vicarage was a one-storey, two-room thatched cottage with a clay floor. Successive glebe terriers between 1764 and 1825 describe the Wharram Percy vicarage as a rather more elegant building than this, although a later terrier of 1853 rather contemptuously recalled the last days of the vicarage, which had been pulled down after the union of the two Wharram parishes in 1834, as 'a mere Cottage with a stable adjoining both covered with thatch.'

The documentation of this vicarage and additional records of its sixteenth-century predecessor were an encouragement to extend the excavation beyond the north boundary of the churchyard, where earlier work had finished after encountering signs of buildings. A trench down the hillside towards the vicarage had been made after the completion of work on House 6 and this had encountered substantial foundations at the foot of the slope.

Since the eighteenth-century vicarage lay north of the churchyard it had always been assumed that the earlier parsonages were situated in the same area, but two discoveries suggest that this may not always have been the case. In late-Saxon and early-medieval times the north boundary of the churchyard seems to have been similar to the present one. To the north of it, a series of post-holes was found that may have formed a major building. Interpretation was hampered by the presence of earlier prehistoric and Romano-British occupation, but it is possible that this was the earliest parsonage, going with the first church on the terrace, or alternatively the outbuildings of an early manor house as yet unidentified.

In the twelfth and thirteenth centuries the site of this building was incorporated in the churchyard, so the parsonage then must have been elsewhere, perhaps at the southern end of the churchyard. In 1983 a trench was dug that found the south boundary of the churchyard and the north boundary of the mill complex. This boundary had remarkable continuity and stability. The earliest feature was a late-Saxon or early-medieval ditch, which was replaced by a medieval stone wall of the fourteenth century, possibly contemporary with the change from mill to fish pond. This was essentially the boundary of the water mill area, as no burials extended into this south-east corner of the churchyard. The nineteenth-century south

boundary of the churchyard was still on the same line, with the posts of its wooden fence in the remains of the stone wall.

Inside the south-east corner of the churchyard a considerable amount of demolition rubbish had been dumped, including good quality building materials and pottery that suggested higher status than a peasant house. The date of this demolition was early fourteenth century, so the rubbish may have come from a twelfth- and thirteenth-century parsonage destroyed in 1327 when Haltemprice Priory was given the advowson. If so, this area was replanned, leaving the pond/churchyard boundary the same but increasing the amount of land available for burials.

Excavation of the churchyard here has not taken place, but the idea of a re-location is supported by the fact that, also in the early fourteenth century, the northern boundary of the churchyard was moved south to its present line and a stone boundary wall was built. Perhaps Haltemprice found that the old parsonage site south of the church was too restricted and built a new one on a larger area to the north, partly over the churchyard, which had spread a long way north by the end of the thirteenth century. Certainly it was a time when a succession of non-resident vicars was followed by resident incumbents. There may also have been further changes of site, since a vacant 'Priesthouse' was given as part of the manorial dower (p. 51) in 1368. In 1440 the vicarage was described as 'against [next to] the church'.

The site of the main buildings of the medieval parsonages could not be excavated until the 1980s since it was situated under the nineteenth-century track passing west of the church. This track could not be diverted until the excavation of the dam area was completed and the heavy machinery required to reconstruct the dam no longer needed to pass up and down. In the 1970s it was possible to excavate only the courtyard to the east, which included outbuildings and the site of the post-medieval parsonage.

The track was of considerable interest for it was the obvious route through the village to the dam and thence to the road across the valley up to the eastern plateau and the three townships in the south of the parish. Haltemprice must have blocked this track when they built the parsonage across it. The course of the track west of the church was then utilized for burials and added to the churchyard, perhaps to make up for the northern part, which the vicarage had just taken over. In its place a terrace road was constructed up the western valley side leading to a second terrace road along the slope above the church, and then continuing down to cross the dam.

This demonstrates another important change in land use, of the type which might well have been carried out by Haltemprice in co-operation with the lord of the manor, their benefactor. It is also early evidence for the diversion of a through road, similar to the work of eighteenth century landowners who diverted roads away from their country houses. This can be seen locally at Birdsall, where the drive used to pass through the village by the house and church but now goes right round the park, while the main road at North Grimston once ran through the present vicarage grounds.

76 *A conjectural reconstruction of a cruck-built tithe barn, burnt down in 1553.*

The site of the late-medieval parsonage is now being excavated, and with one season still to come it is possible in 1989 to offer only an interim interpretation. At first the site appeared to be very confused, with various post-medieval buildings, demolition rubble and large quantities of recent hillwash down the hillside, but two major late-medieval buildings have now been located and uncovered. It is not possible to say yet if these were early enough to be those built by Haltemprice, but their massive nature would go well with the early-fourteenth-century Haltemprice rebuilding or a major reorganization of 1440. They comprise a large building running north-south, which may be interpreted as the cruck barn (76) mentioned in sixteenth-century documents, and to the south a smaller building, aligned east-west, which is likely to have been the sixteenth-century rebuild of the kitchen.

Most important was the finding of a large quantity of burnt grain and possible collapsed roofing inside the barn, together with mid-sixteenth-century pottery. This is therefore likely to be the barn burnt down in the fire of 1553. This is a very important link between the archaeological and historical evidence of a type that now becomes more common in the post-medieval period and will be seen in the eighteenth-century vicarage, the seventeenth-century farmhouse and the 1770s Improving Farm buildings and farmhouses (pp. 107, 111 and 116).

In 1555 the Vicar, William Firby(e), claimed in the ecclesiastical court that his predecessor, Marmaduke Atkinson, who had just moved to the living at Bainton, failed to make good the damage caused by the fire of 1553, and the record includes the depositions of 30 July 1555 from three neighbouring vicars who had assembled at Wharram the previous Friday, together with witnesses from Wharram Grange, Thixendale, Raisthorpe and Towthorpe, to measure the buildings and to determine the character and position of the old and new buildings. They reveal that the burned vicarage had a single room in each of the two storeys of the living quarters, with a kitchen and a barn of six oak 'postes or crokkes [crucks]' under a single thatched roof. The vicars declared that they could see from 'walls which be yet standing' that the new building was 22 yd (20 m) shorter and 2 yd (1.8 m) narrower than the old. Atkinson counterclaimed that he had rebuilt

the vicarage more elaborately than the old, with a parlour and buttery, a double chimney and four bedrooms, one of them 'where guests were laid', and thus, 'that which it lacketh in breadth it hath in height'.

Although the documents suggest that after the fire the parsonage was rebuilt to the north, leading to confusion (see below, p. 122), it was in fact rebuilt to the east. The sixteenth- and seventeenth-century parsonages have been very difficult to interpret because of the sloping ground that led to succeeding buildings being terraced into the slope, and so each destroyed the evidence for earlier structures. In view of the considerable amount of hillwash that has come down over the late-medieval parsonage foundations, it is likely that this was a problem when the vicarage was so close to the slope. The opportunity was therefore taken, after the fire, to rebuild further out on the terrace. Major walls of these buildings have been found but it is not possible to identify them or make a full plan. One of these buildings was a stone-built cellar that is likely to have been a cold store (77) of a type known in the area. This is an interesting stage between the twelfth-century cold store in the Area 10 manor (p. 77) and the aristocratic ice house and the modern refrigerator.

77 Cellar of the seventeenth-century vicarage from the south. This would have been used as a cold store. The feature at the far end would be to allow light into the cellar.

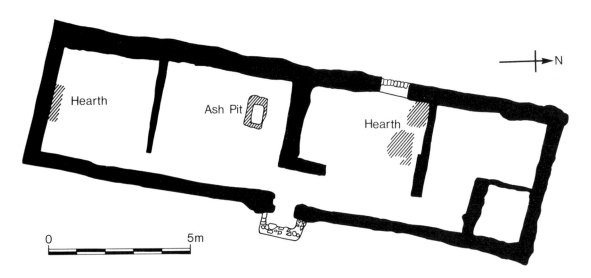

78 *Below: a plan of the excavated eighteenth-century vicarage with the wooden-floored parlour to the left, two central stone-floored rooms with a baffle entrance and service rooms to the right. Above: a conjectural reconstruction of the vicarage based on houses surviving into the nineteenth century at Fimber just to the south of Wharram.*

In the eighteenth century a new parsonage was built still further east, and the main track down to the church then passed to the east of it. It is this period that has been laid out for public display. The parsonage was a long building with a parlour at the south end with a gable fireplace, a baffle entrance in which the doorway was opposite a central chimney stack and further rooms to the north including a kitchen and storehouses, one for coal (**78**). This is another most important correlation

79 *The eighteenth-century vicarage from the south. In the foreground the parlour with the supports for the wooden floor. The walls have been extensively robbed leaving only slight traces of the foundations.*

with documentary evidence. At intervals the bishop required the vicar and church-wardens to make a return (or terrier) of the church's possessions, and that of 1770, repeated in 1825, recorded 'three rooms below stairs with a Pantry annexed, all in one straight Building 19 yd [17 m] long four yards and a half [4 m] wide, 2 rooms flagged and one floored with Deal. Above Stairs four Chambers only of the same dimensions with a false roof without any Garrets (cp. Farm had garrets for male dormitory). The timber of the house consists of Ash Wood and Deal Poles. A stable 11 yard [10 m] by 5 yards [4.5 m]' (**80**).

The 1853 terrier rather contemptuously recalls 'The old Vicarage House was a mere Cottage with a stable adjoining both covered with thatch. The house and stable which were much dilapidated were taken away on the union with Wharram le Street being effected'. The archaeological evidence links very closely with this since in the parlour were found the brick supports for the joists of the wooden floor while in the two other main rooms there were impressions of where the stone flags had been. Underneath the wooden floor of the parlour were found needles, a thimble and marbles that

throw light on the activities of the parson's family on winter evenings. A possible reconstruction, based on local vernacular parallels, of how the eighteenth-century vicarage may have looked is shown in Figure 78.

Towthorpe, Raisthorpe and Thixendale

It is remarkable that, in a parish where four townships have been depopulated, a fifth, Thixendale, should have been unaffected and that Wharram le Street should survive as a village when Wharram Percy succumbed, for there are no differences of soil quality, terrain or climate. Indeed Thixendale is even today notoriously remote and liable to be isolated in winter snow.

The different experiences of the six Wharram townships – with two enclosed by 1500, two others by 1700 and then open fields surviving at Wharram le Street until a Parliamentary enclosure award of 1768 and those of Thixendale until an award of 1795 – demonstrate the important truth that, whatever course the economics of agriculture might suggest at any one time, different and neighbouring landowners took very different views of what should be done. Estates with only one landowner were particularly susceptible to change: at one time the conversion from arable to pasture, and at another time the transformation of pasture and rabbit warrens by the introduction of Improving sheep-and-corn husbandry (p. 115, below). It is a plausible suggestion that it helped to preserve a village if there was a second substantial property owner – in the case of Thixendale and Wharram le Street a monastic house – to balance the interest of the owner of the manorial demesne.

When Beresford first saw St Martin's church in 1948 there was a good deal of visible evidence for the use of the church in the four-and-a-half centuries since the depopulation of the village. Later he examined the parish registers, now in the Borthwick Institute of Historical Research, to count the annual baptisms, marriages and burials (**81**) in an attempt to discover the date of the drastic reductions in population that had reduced Towthorpe and Raisthorpe in their turn to deserted villages.

The registers, with entries going back to 1554, do not consistently distinguish the township concerned, but over an exceptional period (1619–37) when distinctions were made it is significant that only four of the 58 parishioners

A true and perfect Terrier of the [illegible] ands, Rights, or Dues of the Vicar
of Wharram Piercy delivered in at the [illegible] of the Most Rev.d Father in God
Robert by Divine Providence Lord Arch[illegible] of York held at Malton Aug: 13th 1770
Impr: A Vicarage House Consisting [illegible] Rooms below Stairs, with a Pantry
annexed, all in One Streight Building Nineteen Yards long and four Yards & half
Wide, 2 Rooms flagg'd and One floor'd with Deal. Above Stairs four Chambers
only of the Same Dimension, with a false Roof without any Garrets, The
Timber of the House Consists of Ash Wood and Deal Poles
A Stable Eleven Yards long and five Wide
There are twenty Small Ashes upon the Glebe, and Church Yard Fence
in Value by Estimation about Twenty Shillings
The Altar Table is Oak, with a Carpet of Cloth, A Flagon Bason and
Silver Cup, about Seven Ounces in Weight, and two Bells with an Oak Chest
for keeping the Books & Surplice
The Church Yard Fence is repair'd by the Parish
Adjoining to the House is an Orchard and back Yard Planted with Fruit trees
Containing by Estimation with the House Stead One Acre of Land
There are also, two Oxgangs of Arable Meadow and Pasture Land, lying and
being in the Several Fields, Precincts and Territories of Wharram Piercy afores.d
with threescore Sheep gates belonging thereto [illegible]

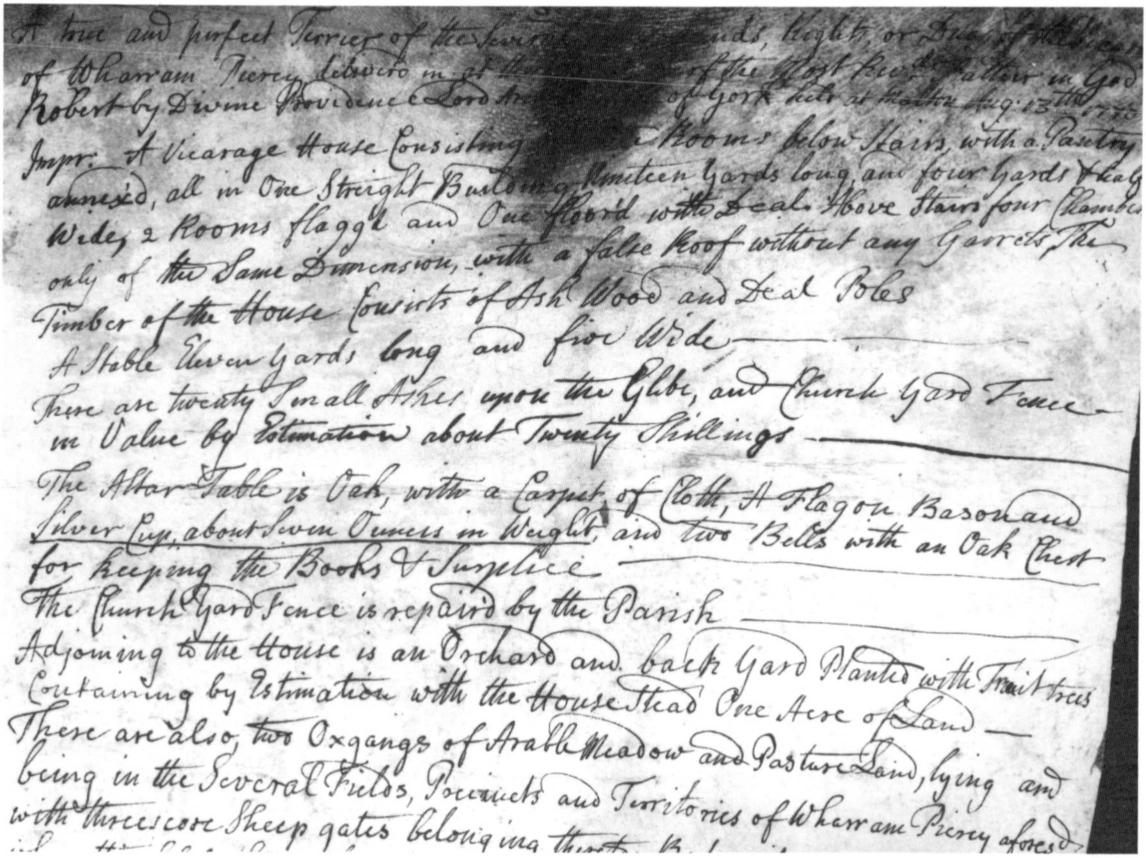

80 *From the Glebe Terrier in 1770 compiled by the vicar and churchwardens. The vicar's assets consisted of his vicarage, small pieces of orchard and garden ground nearby, and some compensation from the landowner for lost grazing rights and the long-indistinguishable selions of two bovates that had been absorbed into the enclosures. The description of the parsonage corresponds with the excavated foundations.*

buried had lived at Wharram Percy; Thixendale, the one village to survive until the present day, contributed 32 and Towthorpe 13. Raisthorpe, with five, was clearly smaller, and the records of the Hearth Tax in 1670–4 show 12 small houses at Towthorpe and 18 at Thixendale but only two at Wharram Percy (**75a** and **b**).

There were virtually no baptisms recorded from Raisthorpe between 1680 and 1710, and it is likely that by this time Raisthorpe had been reduced to a single farm, much as it was described in a survey of a century later:

1100 acres [440 ha] of Land in a Ring fence, no other property interfering., viz about 100 acres [40 hz] of arable, about 300 acres [120 ha] of (rabbit) Warren, about 700 acres [280 ha] in Meadow and Pasture.

Towthorpe entries also become rare in the parish register. There were never more than three in any decade after 1690–9. Later researches in the family papers of the Lloyd-Graemes of Sewerby were to show how their ancestors, the Taylors, had come to dominate that village, steadily absorbing the smaller proprietors' holdings, until the whole parish was cultivated from the two farms (**91**) that still stand side by side beyond the eastern end of the impressive and well-preserved earthworks that cover the walls of the village houses, the manor house and St Catherine's Chapel. A fine estate plan of 1772 shows the shapes of the abandoned crofts fossilized in the paddocks in this area.

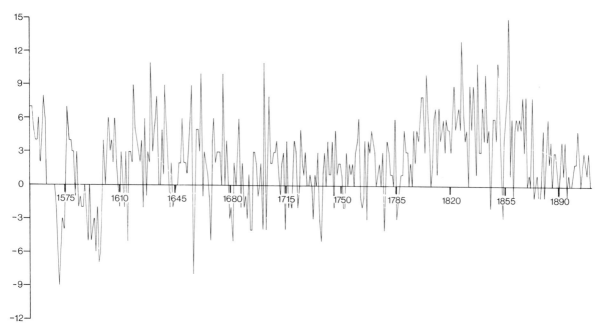

81 *Graph showing the difference in baptisms and burials 1554–1910. There was normally a natural increase by excess of baptisms (the deficit in the period 1580–90 may be due to faulty registration). Baptisms fell off from c. 1690, once Raisthorpe and Towthorpe had come into single ownership. The enlargement of farms by the Improvers brought recovery after 1790. The downturn after 1870 arose from the opening of the new church at Thixendale.*

Gravestones and burials

With the reduction of population in the other townships of the parish the burials recorded in the parish register are dominated by names from Thixendale. Glebe terriers from 1770 to 1825 had recorded the burial fees at one guinea for burials within the church and five shillings in the churchyard. Interior burial had long been the fashion for the wealthier inhabitants. This was probably also true for those clergy whose incumbency of Wharram Percy ended with their deaths, such as Edward Lowthorpe in 1643 and Edward Carlisle in 1668 or those like Joseph Richardson, vicar from 1692 to 1731, who was brought back to be buried there in 1743.

Medieval grave slabs, re-used as building materials, witness the earlier burials of both laymen and clergy although none bears a name. Clerical burials inside the church were encountered during its excavation (p. 64, above), and

requests by laymen for burial within St Martin's church appear in several pre-Reformation wills, not all from Wharram Percy parishioners.

A large, broken grave slab now re-erected in the chancel but once in the nave commemorates the burials in 1687 and 1695 of two children of William Vescy, a principal landowner in Thixendale (**82**). No other interior graves have named slabs, but in 1839 Christiana Harvey was buried in a brick vault just below a wall plaque (now removed to another church) that named three other of her relatives, all Greames, the principal Towthorpe family after the depopulation of that village.

A second wall-plaque (also now removed) to commemorate George Wrangham of Raisthorpe (d. 1791) was erected by his son, but his actual burial, like those of the majority of the parishioners at all periods, was in the churchyard. From the parish registers it is known that there were at least 966 burials between 1570 and 1906. Judging from the surviving tombs and gravestones, the burials of Wrangham's day and subsequently lay only in the south side of the churchyard (see 65).

These 31 graveyard stones have been recorded, analysed and correlated with the parish register's burial entries. None is earlier than 1761. Virtually all the deceased had lived in the parish, and the inscriptions usually located them in one or other of the townships, nearly all from Thixendale although the family of

Megginson, successive Towthorpe tenant farmers in the last two centuries, is well represented. Thus marriages, baptisms and burials continued at St Martin's Church: indeed even after 1870 when Thixendale had its own church some of its villagers still came over the Wolds to services, especially for baptism.

Wharram Percy farms

The final section of this chapter moves back to the ground north of the vicarage. As might be expected, inhabitants of the Wharram Percy farm provided very few of the entries in the parish registers and still fewer gravestones.

The character of agriculture practised from this farm after the depopulation is not well documented. It was reported to the Royal Society's inquiry of 1664–5 that on the high Wolds there was a form of infield-outfield cultivation appropriate to what were then considered poor soils, with only a fraction of a township under arable at any one time.

> ...upon our Wolds which lie near the chalk and flint, their husbandry is different, for

82 Grave slab from the burial of two children of William Vesy in 1687 and 1695.

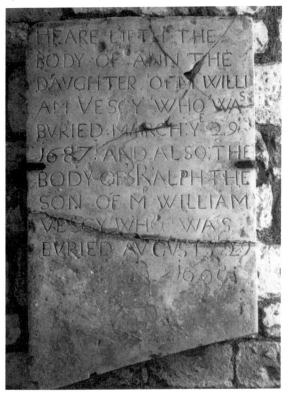

they have in many towns[hips] 7 fields, and the swarth [turf] of one is every year broken for oats and let lie fallow until its turn at 7 years' end, and these 7 are outfields.

Certainly, from the restrictions on the tenant that were imposed in early-seventeenth-century leases Wharram Percy had some enclosures with ditches and hedges, although decay is hinted at: the tenant was

> to mainteyn...all the hedges and ditches sett with quickwood and all the outhedges in and about the grounds and closes of the said manor and pastures...in all places where quickwood hath bene sett and nowe decayed

> ...not to plowe any part other than such as have bene used for tillage nowe or within xx [20] years last past, (and in any case not to exceed 100 acres [40 ha] of the inclosed ground and 400 [160 ha] of the pasture at large).

Any arable cultivation that was taking place was, of course, no longer in separate selions since all but the tiny, two-oxgang glebe holding had come into single ownership. Judging from the confused language of an early-seventeenth-century terrier, the glebe selions had been quietly swallowed up, and the vicar and churchwardens who compiled it might have done better if they had confessed (as their successors were obliged to in 1663) that the selions, each once with its boundary mark, had become indistinguishable. Indeed, even in the mid sixteenth century, witnesses who could recall a time when crops had been taken from the glebe nevertheless implied that the vicar could no longer do so:

> yf the vicar of Wharom percye for the tyme beinge mighte be permytted to plowe his arable grounde throughe the Feldes as other towneships therabouts do, his two oxgangs of Lande were hable to beare...xvi [16] lode of Corne..

Common rights and communal cultivation had gone, and it was just that sort of Wolds landscape described by Alan Harris as 'physically open but technically enclosed'.

The earliest documentary evidence for the character and contents of a farmstead at Wharram Percy is an inventory of March 1699 attached to the will of the tenant farmer, William Botterell. It was clearly much more

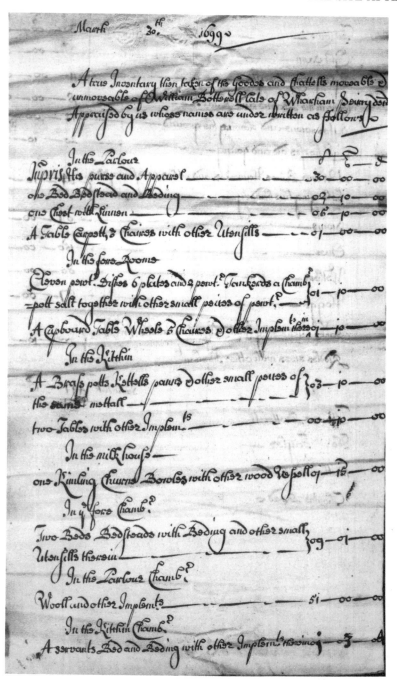

83 *From the 'true Inventary (sic) taken of the Goodes and Chattells moveable & immoveable of William Botterell late of Wharham Percy' on 30 March 1699. The valuation proceeded room by room – Parlour, 'fore Roome', 'Kitchin' and* *'milk house' on the ground floor (the three hearths of Figure. 75; three rooms, and the three chambers on the upper floor; then to the livestock, the grain in the barn and the field, and the farm gear.*

substantial than a medieval house for the goods that the inventory valued were located in four downstairs rooms and three more on the second storey. These were named as follows (83): on the ground floor were 'the Parlour', 'the fore Roome', 'the Kitchin' and 'the milk house', and above them a 'fore Chamber', a 'Parlour Chamber' and a 'Kitchin Chamber', the last containing 'a Servant's Bed and Beding (sic)'.

Although by far the largest component of the valuation of stock and implements was a sheep flock (worth £257) and there was 'Wooll and other Implements' in the chamber over the Parlour worth £51, mixed husbandry had certainly already returned. There was corn worth £18 in the chamber alongside the wool and in a barn and 'Oates sowne' worth £12; alongside the milk cows were eight oxen, and in the barn 'A Wain [waggon], Plows, Harrows and other necessaryes belonging husbandry'.

The remains of this farmhouse were exposed during the 1989 season of excavations, complementing the documentary evidence. They also showed that the tenant farmer and his neighbour, the vicar (p. 106, above), had houses of very similar size and plan. The excavated remains of the farm lay under those of Sir Charles Buck's rebuilding (1775–9, below) but on a slightly different alignment. Its rooms extended in a single line, in the medieval manner. At the southern end there was a room – presumably the parlour – with a fireplace in its gable end nearest the vicarage. The impression of joists for supporting a wooden floor could still be seen in the earth. Next to it were a stone-flagged entrance hall and a path leading up to it between a yard to the north, overlooked by the kitchen and a garden to the south that would have been overlooked from the parlour window. The entrance led into the 'fore room' and kitchen, both of which were also flagged. The final room in the row, the milk house, had a brick floor. The barn mentioned in the inventory would have been a separate building and, if it lay on the more workaday north side of the farmhouse, it would have been the predecessor of the range of outbuildings added in the enlargement of 1775–79 (below, p. 115).

The same season's excavation also found a few undisturbed remains of a still earlier farmhouse. It will be remembered that there had been a regular line of crofts on the eastern side of the village green (34), so that this building could have been sited as the last in that row. Unfortunately its plan could not be recovered without removing the foundations of the later farms, which were intended to be preserved for possible display, but it was noticed that the ground on which these farmhouses rested was the result of an artificial levelling to counteract the natural slope of the valley side. This 'raft' of chalk was similar to that which had been created to support the church a little further up the valley (p. 58, above).

The beginning of work to create the latest of the three farmsteads revealed in the excavations can be exactly dated, thanks to the preservation of accounts rendered to the landlord's agent. On 23 August 1773 Sir Charles Buck came from Hanby Grange, his Lincolnshire home, to meet the mason who was going to supervise the extensive building operations planned for his Wharram estate, which included a new farmhouse out on the Bella Pasture that lay on the Wharram le Street side of Wharram Percy township (12) and had already been detached from the main farm and worked by a series of tenants living in Wharram le Street.

With a series of absentee landlords, the day-by-day working of the land on the Buck Estate had always been in the hands of the tenant farmers, restricted only by covenants in their lease such as those imposed in the late sixteenth century to limit the destruction of pasture by an extension of tillage. A list of tenants on the Buck estate at Wharram Percy, Bella Pasture, Wharram le Street and Wharram Grange in the mid eighteenth century can be seen in Figure 84.

The changes in husbandry practice in the eighteenth century that are usually summed up as 'Improvement' depended heavily on the enthusiasm of a landlord since they called for substantial investment. The tenant farmer would expect to achieve greater efficiency and increase his earnings but the landlord would expect a reward for his investment by an increase in the tenant's rent, whether from the sitting tenant or an incomer. John Monkman, the tenant of Wharram Percy, remained undisturbed: he had been there since at least 1746, when his eldest son, William, was baptized at the church. William eventually succeeded his father in the tenancy, and after his death in 1786 Francis, another brother, took over the farm and remained there for 20 years.

An important element in new husbandry

84 *The two Wharrams from the rental of Lady Buck's estate, undated but about 1729–50. The two Pinders and Read were joint tenants of the single farm at Wharram Percy, where Bellow (Bella) pastures were rented by Thomas Wharham (sic) of Wharram le Street. Wharram Grange, in Wharram le Street parish, was also a single farm. In contrast, Wharram le Street village had three tenants with a substantial 'arrable farme', and seven with smaller farms; nine cottages brought the total number of village houses to 19.*

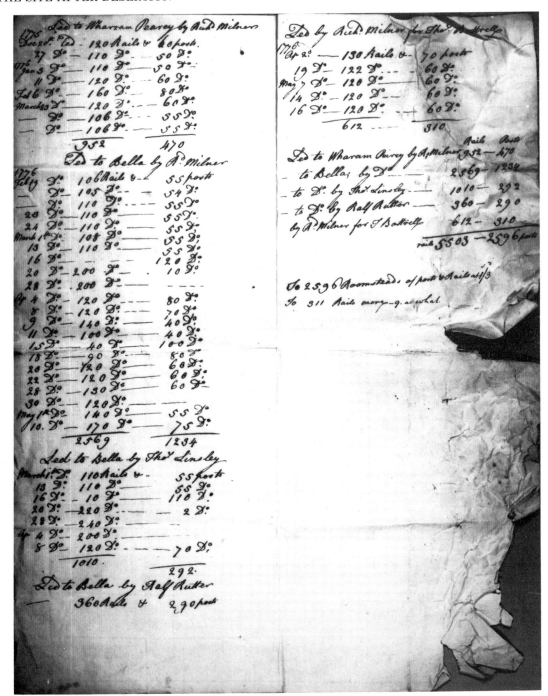

85 *Agricultural Improvement at Wharram Percy and Bella 1775–7, from accounts rendered to Sir Charles Buck for work done. This leaf of the accounts runs from December 1775 to April 1776 and is for carriage of wooden posts and rails for fencing the new fields at Bella and Wharram Percy.*

practices was the provision of larger farm buildings, such as barns, but a landlord who took some pride in the appearance of his estate often took the opportunity to rebuild the tenant's farmhouse. This was not simply paternalism, for, as can be seen from the inventories of their contents, rooms within the farmers' houses at Wharram Percy and Wharram Grange were used partly as store rooms, and increasingly the tenants' accommodation was shared with their farm servants and labourers (below, p. 119).

The best-known advocates of agricultural improvement in the Wolds are William Marshall, author of *The Rural Economy of Yorkshire* (1788) and Isaac Leatham, who compiled his *General View of the Agriculture of the East Riding* for the Board of Agriculture in 1794. Locally much credit is given to Sir Christopher Sykes of Sledmere, although it is Sir Tatton Sykes (died 1863) whose monument dominates the Wolds with an inscription proclaiming that he converted the Wolds from rabbit warrens and rough pasture into good quality wheatlands. In fact the Middletons of Birdsall, the Grimstons of Neswick, the Stricklands of Boynton and the Constables of Burton Constable were as avid for Improvement.

In Sledmere there were proprietors other than the Sykes who had common rights, so that there, as elsewhere in England, it was necessary to obtain an Act of Parliament (1776) to extinguish these and allow the creation of individually-owned fields. On them, with the abolition of fallow, an occupier could introduce new rotations and crops such as clover, turnips and sanfoin. The consolidation of scattered selions into fields was also seen as a substantial economy in working the land as well as a prerequisite for innovation.

Private Acts of Parliament of this sort or equivalent formal agreements preceded the enclosure of Wharram le Street (1766) and Thixendale (1794) but in the three other Wharram townships there was no need for an Act before changes were made, since each had only a single owner. Nevertheless substantial physical changes had to be made, involving much capital expenditure. The new fields had to be lined with ditches, banks and quickset hedges before rotations could be introduced and the existing sheep-corn husbandry made more productive. The increase in the arable yields necessitated more farm labourers and

larger farm dormitories and kitchens to house them. Other buildings were needed as stockyards for wintering flocks and herds, as well as to house the farm equipment and draught animals, and to store corn, hay, straw and fodder. Streams are few in the Wolds, and to obtain water for the livestock deep wells had to be dug, as with the digging and clay lining of a 112-ft (33.6-m) well at Bella farm in 1776. The Wharram Percy farm of the same date was low lying and could be supplied by building a conduit from springs further up the valley. The elaborate stone-lined conduit (48) was found during the excavation of the churchyard and the vicarage and its line is now marked out on the ground.

It is possible to follow the progress of Buck's building works on his Wharram estate, for by chance a thick bundle of accounts and receipts survived in the office of Buck's local agent, a Malton solicitor, and is now in the North Yorkshire County Record Office. They are written on small, loose sheets but the type of expenditure is identical with that tabulated for Thixendale between 1796 and 1799 in the Sykes estate day book after all the proprietors but one had been bought out and an enclosure Act obtained.

The Buck accounts show that, between December 1775 and May 1776, 2,596 timber posts and 5,503 rails were delivered to Wharram for fences and 500 ash plants were purchased to line them. During this period foundations for new buildings were being dug at Wharram Percy, and 80,000 bricks were brought from Little Driffield to build at Bella. Masons were still at work there on walling, tiling, corbels, coping and paving when the bundle of accounts ends in 1779, but work on both farms would seem to have been completed when Sir Charles and Lady Buck visited in October 1780.

The accounts have dimensions and descriptions of building work: for example at Wharram Percy six stone arches, granary steps, a barn 38 ft 4 in. (30 m) by 15 ft 2 in. (4.6 m), and a stable with joists 30 ft 6 in. (9.3 m) by 20 ft (6 m) with doors, frames and lintels. There were 90 ft (27 m) of plain plinth 'in ye granary'. The Bella barn was a little smaller, with a roof span of 80 ft 9 in. (24.6 m) by 16 ft 10 in. (5.13 m) (85).

We have very little record of the agriculture practised at this time from the new farm. The inventory of William Monkman's possessions in 1786 is terse and did not proceed room-by-room. A flock of 1,310 sheep dominated his stock: he had 20 horses and as many cattle. The crops valued in the fields were turnips, corn and hay.

However, the architecture of Bella and Wharram Grange farms (which survive) and of the demolished Wharram Percy farm is as much the expression of changed agricultural practices as are the arrival of hedged fields and the massive extension of arable husbandry over the former pastures and warrens. A survey made in 1805, when Lord Middleton was about to take a long head-lease of the former Buck estate, shows the number of fields that had been created:

Farm	Number of closes #
Wharram Percy 902¾ acres (365.3 ha)	16*
Bella 532 acres (215.3 ha)	18
Wharram Grange 254½ acres (102.9 ha) *293 acres (118.2 ha)	18 *20

excluding lane sides and small areas of homesteads and paddocks
* two closes formerly part of Wharram Percy had been taken over by Wharram Grange farm: their area was 38½ acres (15.6 ha)

Three years later Lord Middleton prescribed the future rules of Improved husbandry for these fields: at Bella the Old Tillage close was already in a four-course rotation of turnips, corn, clover and wheat. The other closes were to be pared and burnt then converted into tillage, afterwards being cropped with turnips, corn and then turnips before going into the same four-course rotation as Old Tillage. Wharram Grange was to retain eight closes of 'ancient tillage' and ten of 'ancient pasture'. At Wharram Percy the tenant was to continue five closes as ancient pasture but convert two to (permanent) tillage and another to nine-course husbandry, while bringing five closes of ancient tillage into six-course husbandry and three others into three-course rotations.

The character of the new Wharram Percy farm is also revealed in a valuation made in November 1830 after agricultural depression had brought bankruptcy to John Cattle, tenant since 1817. Lord Middleton noted in his diary at this time, when he was thinking of purchasing the estate, that the farm buildings would need much attention. The bankrupt's valuation was not concerned with the quality of the landlord's buildings but it did list them when assigning the contents: there were five stacks of wheat, six stacks of oats and two stacks of hay; there had to be accommodation for four waggons, one cart, four ploughs and 12 harrows as well as an unelaborated entry for a 'Machine'.

The oxen of 1699 had been replaced by 13 horses, and the extension of arable under the new husbandry practices was marked by the increase in the labour force. It was no longer a farm of family labour and one resident servant: besides the two bedsteads in the 'Servant Girl's

86 *View from the north of the 1775–9 farmhouse. The main living part is on the top right with the farm labourers' kitchen, with its ash pit and oven, in the left foreground. Behind, the service rooms are divided by brick partitions.*

Room' were the eight in the 'Men Servants Garett'. A large bedroom of this kind survives at Bella Farm (built, as we have seen, at the same time) as well as at Wharram Grange and the two farms in Wharram le Street village.

The schedules compiled by the census enumerators 11 years after Cattle's bankruptcy confirm a resident labour force of young unmarried men in all these farms: nine at Wharram Percy, seven at Bella, six at Burdale, 15 at Raisthorpe and 19 at the two farms that shared the fields of Towthorpe. Clearly, labour-intensive cultivation had returned to the parish yet, significantly, without a resurrection of any of these four villages.

Excavating Wharram Percy farmhouse

The Wharram Percy farmhouse improved by Buck has been fully excavated (89). It was constructed of chalk in the traditional manner, but on the west and south sides, facing the road and the church, the wall was brick-faced in English garden-wall bond (see 100). The back

87 *View from the south-west of the 1775–9 farmhouse, with the farmer's kitchen in the foreground and the labourer's kitchen in the background.*

east wall was made of sandstone, faced with ashlar, which shows the fashion of the period. While nowadays a stone wall might seem to be of higher quality than brick, at the end of the eighteenth century it was fashionable to build in brick.

The western half of the farmhouse contained a parlour with a wooden floor, to the south (like the parsonage) an entrance hall and then a front kitchen for the family; this had a fireplace and oven with an ashpit in front. Behind, in the eastern half of the farmhouse, was a series of service rooms and a back kitchen also with a fireplace, oven and ashpit. This would have been for the use of the farm labourers, who lived in and also had their dormitory accommodation in the first floor, as in the later Wharram Percy Farm house (86-7).

To the north of the farmhouse, on a different alignment, there were a series of four buildings round a courtyard. The south range still survives, converted into cottages, and excavation has shown that it originally had wider doorways for cattle. It was faced on the west and south sides with bricks in English garden-wall bond. The east range had a chalk-built east wall, but its west wall was missing. A single

88 *The south end of the west range showing the chalk wall foundations and cobbled floor, possibly a stable (1775–7). Underneath, on a different alignment, are medieval buildings.*

sandstone padstone suggested that this was the last survivor of a number, of which all the rest had been robbed. It is therefore possible that this building was open-fronted on to the court-yard in the tradition of many surviving farm buildings on the Wolds, and that it would have been the structure with six stone arches mentioned in the building accounts.

The north range was very extensively robbed and disturbed by later gardening activities from the cottages but it comprised two buildings on either side of a main entrance, the access to which cut across several medieval tofts. The west range was better preserved as part of it was sealed under a nineteenth century track. It was chalk-built but faced with brick on the west side and at each end. Of considerable interest was the fact that, over the period of about 75 years during which these farm buildings were in use, the range was rebuilt

and modified at least three times. This shows the changing farming practices of the late eighteenth and early nineteenth centuries that necessitated new types of farm buildings (**88**).

The Improved Wharram Percy farm and its courtyard outbuildings appear on a large-scale estate plan made for Lord Middleton in 1836 soon after his tenancy had been converted into a freehold. Five years later the census returns confirm the residence of unmarried farm labou-rers in its dormitory. They also confirm that the vicarage no longer existed, but by the time of the next census in 1851 an even more drastic change had taken place. The Wharram Percy farm had been demolished and the 1851 6-in (15-cm) Ordnance Survey plan shows earthworks in its place. Instead, farming operations were now conducted from a new site 1 mile (1.6 km) to the south-west where farm buildings known as High House had been constructed earlier in the century, probably at the expense of Lord Middleton. Isolated groups of buildings of this kind, usually known as High Barns, were a feature of the Improvers' farms in the Wolds,

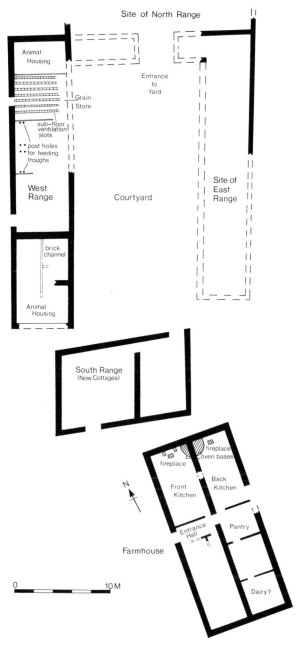

89 *Wharram Percy Improving Farm (1775–9). The plan of the excavated farmhouse with its division into the farmer's and the farm labourers' accommodation. To the north were the courtyard outbuildings. Of the four ranges there were substantial remains only of the west; the south range was converted about 1850 into the cottages that survive today.*

and several survive; some have been surveyed as part of the Wharram parishes survey (**90**).

The reason for the change of site, which brought the village field nearly back to the deserted state of the early sixteenth century, is undocumented. Perhaps it was realized that the confined space in the valley bottom left no room for further outbuildings. Unlike Wharram le Street, Thixendale and Bella, where Enclosure Acts had created new access roads to or past their farms, the road to Wharram Percy was still the steep and deeply-cut hollow way, the ancient Towthorpe way, and in 1847 the estate may have feared a worsening of access once the valley between the two Wharrams was occupied by the Malton to Driffield railway that had just begun to be built. Trains came close to the farm before they entered the long tunnel, but they could not be boarded there; the nearest station for passengers and goods was named 'Wharram' but could be reached only circuitously via Bella and Wharram le Street.

The High House outbuildings were partially incorporated in extensive enlargements but a new farm house was built, taking the name of the demolished Wharram Percy farm. Set on a plateau and surrounded by a windbreak plantation of trees typical of the many isolated Wolds farms (**92**), it was a very genteel residence, clearly designed for a tenant farmer of substance. It has a pretentious south facade (**11**), a garden and a shrubbery, but the interior is a mixture of a gentleman's house and a working farm. The accommodation was firmly divided into three parts (**93**): in the main section of the house, with reception rooms and a grand staircase leading up to the family bedrooms, was the farmer's accommodation; in the south side there was a large communal kitchen for the farm labourers with a separate stair leading down from their dormitory where they lived as they did in the farm that had just been demolished; and a third stair led to a small room for the female servants.

In the census of 1861 there were 13 male labourers and four female servant residents: the farmworkers' dormitories at the Wharram Percy farms and at Bella explain why at every census between 1801 and 1841 there were never fewer than 30 inhabitants recorded in the township. However, the increase of 136 persons between 1841 and 1851 is a freak. The railway navvies came in 1847, and 21 temporary huts for workmen and their families, described as

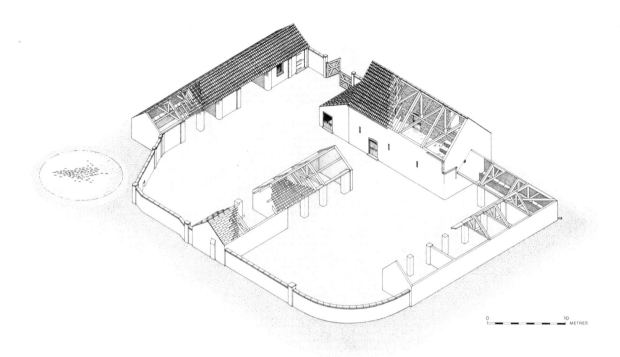

90 *Towthorpe high barn west. Isometric draw-ing showing the early-nineteenth-century enclos-ure with a barn on the right, a series of open sheds in two enclosures, outside them to the left was a dewpond, a typical feature of the late-eighteenth-century Improving farms.*

91 *Towthorpe barn and a granary over arched wagon sheds with a gable date stone 1831. In the background is the double farmhouse.*

92 *1971 oblique air photograph of the mid-nineteenth-century Wharram Percy farm set in its windbreak of trees typical of the Wolds. Wharram is close to the edge of the Wolds, and the Vale of York can be seen in this view, looking west.*

120

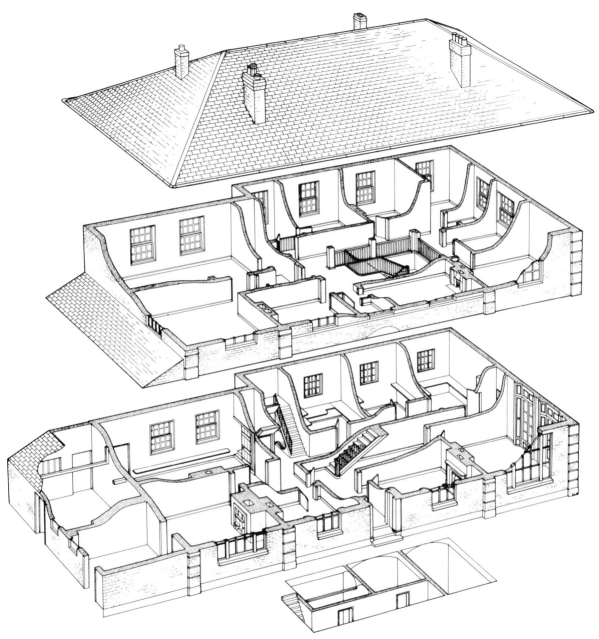

93 *The present Wharram Percy farmhouse built on a site remote from the present village about 1850. Split isometric drawing showing more clearly than fig. 89 the tripartite accommodation for the farmer and his family, the farm labourers and the female servants.*

'railway cottages' in the 1851 census, temporarily inflated the population. These numbers were not equalled until the latter years of the excavation when a census night would have found more than 100 temporary residents in the Low House cottages and in tents, caravans and dormobiles spread over the south western crofts of the village.

Demolition of the farm at the old site was not quite total: the south range of the outbuildings was retained and, after a second storey had been added in English bond brickwork, it was converted into three cottages, named Low House, where successive censuses from 1851 onwards would show agricultural labourers to be living. The cottages have survived to form the headquarters for the research project, providing dormitories, offices, kitchen and common rooms.

It is one of the ironies of the project that as it was known that the parsonage was demolished between the parish amalgamation of 1834 and the first estate map of 1836, the earthworks of the demolished farmhouse on the 1851 Ordnance Survey map were interpreted as the remains of the parsonage. This seemed to be confirmed by the sixteenth-century documen-

tary evidence that the later parsonage was built to the north of the earlier one. In the 1950s, when the farmhouse foundations were first uncovered, there was no thought that an Improving farm had been built on the terrace, the assumption being made that it was incorporated in the present Wharram Percy farm.

When the post-medieval vicarage was found further south, and it became clear that the foundations in the south cottage garden were the eighteenth-century farmhouse, it transpired that the Milners had always known where the parsonage was and were puzzled that the archaeologists had placed it elsewhere. This shows that local traditions should not always be cast aside because of academic arrogance.

7

A site for the public

The main aim of the Department of the Environment, and now English Heritage, since the site was taken into care has been to build on the 40 years of research in order to present to the general public a medieval village in as many different aspects as possible and to supplement the partial impression of daily life gained from visiting castles, religious houses and other major buildings that were used by only a small fraction of the medieval population. Wharram was an ideal site as it complements the wide range of sites and monuments in care, originally of a much higher social status, that can be visited in eastern Yorkshire.

Whilst the excavation has been in progress work has steadily continued on consolidating the ruined buildings, marking out above ground those which have been destroyed and trying to interpret the earthworks to the public. In addition, considerable attention has been given to the ecological evidence, and attempts have been made to recreate a series of medieval and post-medieval features that will give the visitor a complete picture of non-archaeological elements in the local historic landscape.

Presentation

The first important conservation work was the consolidation of the fabric of the church, which was in a dangerous state following the collapse of the west face of the tower in 1959. This was carried out between 1970 and 1977 when the decayed nineteenth-century roof of the nave was removed, a concrete ring beam put around the walls to hold them together and the walls consolidated. It was possible to retain the roofs of the chancel and the porch. Almost everywhere in the church the visitor will see clear evidence for the successive periods in its development. Although it is unfortunate that the tower collapsed, the consolidated ruin is an instructive visual aid: many people, seeing an ashlar wall made of squared blocks, would think that the wall was solidly built of dressed

94 *The consolidated ruin of the church of St Martin with the east end marked out and the gravestones in the foreground.*

stone as a brick building is of bricks. In fact ashlar walls are rarely built in this way: the carefully finished facing is normally only the outer skin round a rubble core. This is clearly visible in the broken north and south walls of the tower, which still stand 44 ft 6 in (13.6 m) high (**94**).

Except for parts of the south aisle, where the foundations protrude above ground level, most of the demolished walls of the church are either robbed or survive only below ground level. These have therefore been marked out outside by outlining the outer faces of the ashlar walls with York stone slabs set on edge, infilling the area of the rubble core with Breedon gravel. Inside the church the earliest stone nave and chancel were marked out with stone slabs and a floor of Breedon gravel. It is hoped that this will give the visitor a general impression of the expansion of the parish church from the small pre-conquest stone church to the larger twelfth-century building, with its extended chancel and aisles, which then contracted to its present size following the progressive abandonment of four of the five villages in the parish (95).

The only other standing structure on the village site is the row of three agricultural labourers' cottages. Fortunately the roof is sound and has needed only slight repair. In particular it has been possible to retain the riven laths on which the pantiles were hung in the mid nineteenth century. A lot of air comes through, but it is this ventilation that has kept the roof in such good condition. The rest of the woodwork has been repaired, and the windows, with their lattice panes, have been replaced. In 1990 it is intended to investigate the interior of the building and possibly expose to the public any traces that remain of the 1770s farm range and any earlier features. The only other structure that it has been possible to consolidate is the seventeenth-century cold store of the parsonage. As this was mainly made of mudstone it is hoped that it will survive in the open air.

95 *Model of the ruined church as presented to the visitor with the demolished east end, north-east chapel and north aisle marked out in the grass. Viewed from the north.*

The parish church was built mainly of sandstone, brought from quarries some miles away at the foot of the Wold scarp at Birdsall or North Grimston, which it is possible to conserve and display. All other buildings, including the twelfth-century manor house, were built largely of chalk quarried from the areas where the structures were built. It is not possible to consolidate and display these chalk foundations for, although they were perfectly sound (as buildings) when they were constructed, this was only because they were kept dry and protected from the weather. Once uncovered, especially after being buried in the ground and saturated by water for 500 years, the chalk is very friable and it cracks and powders after frost. In any case most of the walls of the peasant houses were quite slight and not complete, so even if they had been made of a durable stone it would have been difficult to consolidate and present them.

It was therefore decided that the only way to try and present the peasant houses and the Area 10 manor house to the visitor would be to mark them out in the same way as the church foundations, with York slabs outlining a Breedon gravel core. As the complete laying out of all the periods excavated would only be confusing, and there is some uncertainty about the plans of some of the buildings, only a few

basic periods were marked out, different periods being shown by the infilling of the walls either with Breedon or Hovingham gravel.

In Area 6 with its straightforward sequence of peasant houses three main periods were laid out, according to the interpretation of the 1970s. Two thirteenth-century small houses on different alignments were marked out, overlain by two parallel long-houses. Although this gives a misleading impression of the regularity of the walls, it does demonstrate the general size of the medieval peasant long-house, with its main living room with central hearth, cross passage and lower end for cattle, showing how the gentle slope of the site has been utilized. It also gives a very good impression of the size of a medieval peasant house, whose living quarters were much larger than many people imagine with about the same floor area as an average modern council house (**colour plate 3**).

In Area 10, with its complex sequence, the three main periods have been marked out showing the fundamental changes in site use. Firstly, the twelfth-century manor-house solar block has been marked out with its wall, doorway, chimney support and the three pillar bases for posts holding up the upper floor. Secondly, the area to the south has been left rough as it would have been after the late thirteenth-century quarrying. An attempt has been made to create hollows representing the main individual quarries but this has been hampered by the continued grazing of the field. Thirdly, the first of the fourteenth-century peasant houses has been marked out. As the later buildings were over the quarries they would have been hard to lay out with the quarries marked out as hollows, but it is hoped that the three main periods shown will inform the public about the development of the site.

On the terrace, the post-medieval parsonage walls have been marked out with York stone

96 *Presentation of the terrace. The 1983 scheme for laying out the archaeological remains on the terrace with the courtyard farm of 1775–9 on the left, the medieval and post-medieval vicarages in the centre, and the church to the right.*

outlines and Hovingham gravel core infill. The inside of the building has been filled with Breedon gravel to differentiate the inside and outside. (It was not possible on the plateau to have large expanses of gravel because of the grazing animals.) The east range of the 1770s Improving Farm courtyard has been laid out in similar fashion, but, as more of the west range survives, it is being marked out in a variety of materials to represent the original structure. It is hoped in 1990 and 1991 to mark out in a similar hybrid fashion the 1770s farm house and the late medieval parsonage kitchen and

barn. The terrace will therefore present to the public a multiperiod sample of the site (**96**).

In the early 1980s a scheme of display panels was developed using stainless steel, with incised lettering and designs infilled with coloured enamels to depict the different periods on the plans and reconstruction drawings (**97**).

The display panels at the church and the peasant houses, and eventually at the parsonage and farm, are fairly straightforward. It was hoped that these basic display panels would be backed up by a general exhibition near the cottages, setting the village in its wider background and explaining the various parts of

97   *Steel plaque of Area 10 Manor House.*

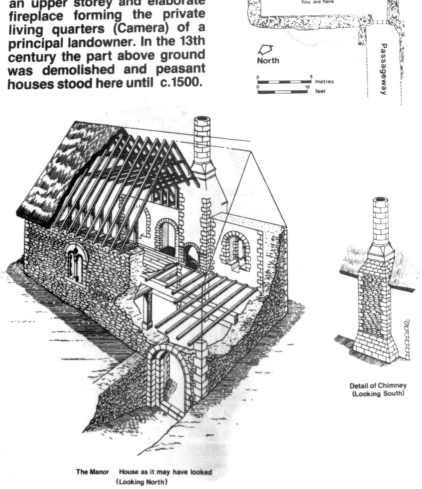

The grass platform marks the area where a 12th century stone manor house was excavated between 1955 & 1957. It consisted of a deep basement with an upper storey and elaborate fireplace forming the private living quarters (Camera) of a principal landowner. In the 13th century the part above ground was demolished and peasant houses stood here until c.1500.

Cellar

You are here

North

Passageway

The Manor   House as it may have looked
(Looking North)

Detail of Chimney
(Looking South)

the site in more detail. Hopefully the current survey of the needs for a final display after 1990 will result in a background display, an essential support for the display panels on each part of the site. For the visiting public, and especially visiting school parties, English Heritage, in their Education series, have produced a general introduction to the site with a suggested tour. The consolidated and marked out areas of the site form a very small part of the Guardianship area. Only 6 per cent of the 38-acre (15.4-ha) site will have been excavated, the rest comprising the main earthworks of the tofts and crofts and the north manor house. The explanation of these earthworks presents a much greater challenge than the marked out foundations, which should be readily visible and identifiable through the information on the display boards.

Ecology

The multidisciplinary nature of the research project has always included environmental evidence. Archaeologically, little of this survives on the chalk, but it is well preserved in the waterlogged deposits in the valley bottom, which have been investigated under the dams. To amplify this, ecological work has been undertaken during the last 20 years.

This has comprised four main projects: a survey to identify the plant and animal communities that still exist in the parish and on adjacent areas of the Wolds; historical research on past fauna, flora and land management by an examination of manuscript records that describe the plants, animals and agriculture of past centuries; reconstruction where possible to restore elements of the historic landscape and thus give visitors some appreciation of an earlier environment; and creative maintenance to manage some areas for their wildlife value and to add to the visual amenity of the site (and hence its attractiveness for visitors).

These reconstructed habitats will also provide an indication of the range of species that were probably present in the past, particularly for those groups of organisms and habitat types for which no surviving examples exist in today's landscape and for which no archaeological remains have been found.

As many of the present local woods have an impoverished flora, as a result of high forestry management, information has been utilized from a wider survey. This has been linked with a study of species-rich hedges on the Wolds

and the evidence from charcoal found in the excavations to indicate the species that once formed the understorey of bushes under the tall trees of the medieval woods (p. 68). This has enabled a small medieval wood to be planted that will be managed as coppice with oak standards. A scheme has been established to monitor the growth of the trees and shrubs as well as the changes in ground flora over time. It is hoped that many of the associated species of insects will re-colonize. A large number of hawthorn and some blackthorn bushes have become established in the valley and on the hillsides to afford good nesting habitats for woodland-edge birds.

To what extent live hedges were present in the medieval period or whether fences or dead hedges were used to separate the tofts and crofts is a hard question to answer. A programme of hedge planting along the boundaries of the guardianship area has included a wide range of single- and mixed-species hedges to see how different types survive. The reconstructed pond has already become surprisingly rich and varied in fauna. The island provides a secure home for several wildfowl that act as a focus of visitor interest.

The tall grassland areas approximate in their insect life to the hay crops that were grown on some of the fields. Although the flora of the plateau has been much changed by the use of fertilizers and herbicides, the steep slopes have not been managed and have changed little from when they were grazed in medieval times. The infertile soil favours wild flowers, grasshoppers and butterflies.

The 1770 terrier and the 1836 Estate map describe and show the vicarage orchard on the slope between the parsonage and the stream. In the 1950s some decayed apple trees were still present in this area, and the Milners transferred Bullace suckers to their cottage garden in 1944. These have now become large trees that provide a considerable amount of fruit. The last apple tree fell during storms in the 1960s, but suckers have come up from one of these to form a bush. A programme of planting eighteenth-century varieties of apple to recreate the orchard in the same widely spaced pattern that once existed is now in progress. A soft fruit garden is also planned by the stream.

Until recently, many fine ash trees dotted the site, the remains of planting by the Middletons when they acquired the property in the early nineteenth century. Now, after 150 years, most of these are beyond their prime and several have fallen or become unsafe in the last 40 years. As tree roots damage the earthworks and the archaeological remains underneath, there has been no replanting on the village site itself. Instead, around the margins of the site, four newly-established clumps of Ash, Beech, Hornbeam and Common Lime represent the style of landscape planting of the eighteenth century.

These plantations are, of necessity, much smaller than would have been the case then, as can be seen from the examples dotted about the skyline round Wharram, but they provide a very different form of planting from the medieval wood in the valley bottom. Elsewhere on the site, alder plantations have been put on two valley bottom sites, and the marshy area below the cottages has been planted to illustrate rural pollarding.

The aim therefore for the 1990s is to present a picture of the Wharram landscape in all its aspects, so that the visitor can appreciate the archaeological, historical and ecological features of the site, in all their variations throughout the centuries of its settlement, as a unity.

8

Forty years in the field

In North and East Yorkshire a retrospective of 40 years in the field has distinguished precedents: 40 years was the duration of the pioneer examination of many aspects of history in a single parish: Danby – also with a deserted medieval village – that formed the subject of Canon Atkinson's *Forty Years in a Moorland Parish*; and including the area of the two Wharram parishes, Mortimer's *Forty Years' Researches in British and Saxon Burial Mounds of East Yorkshire*.

After 40 years at Wharram some assertions can be confidently made: there was no need for scepticism, the earthworks at Wharram Percy were from a medieval village, and the house sites had not been occupied as dwellings since the early-sixteenth-century depopulation. A longer period of survival than at Wharram Percy has occurred at Towthorpe, where the more complex groups of earthworks represent its buildings at the late-seventeenth-century depopulation. Documentation places the desertion of the less well-preserved site of Raisthorpe in the same period. By its survival, alone of the five townships, Thixendale poses a crucial question but one not yet wholly answered: how do neighbouring communities, placed so similarly, have such a different fate?

Wharram le Street, its very name suggesting some original larger unity, 'Wharram', had an experience half way between survival and desertion; it is one of the several thousand English villages now recognized as 'shrunken'. Its enclosed fields did not pass into pasture but were worked from the outlying Grange as well as from the two ancient farms in the village street.

Thus, the present conclusions about the chronology of settlement in the area once thought to have been only that of a medieval village are of more ancient but shifting use. Although excavation suggested forest clearance in Neolithic times the first evidence for the form of an agricultural landscape is of Iron Age trackways, buildings and enclosures, one at least of these trackways continuing as a medieval road. This landscape was not modified, as it was at Wharram le Street, by a Roman villa and a Roman road. In this landscape the equivalent of a 'village' was a group of dwellings, probably not more than six, which did not always occupy the same position.

In the Saxon period the 'village' was still a shifting group of dwellings matched by others elsewhere in the 1,500 acres (600 ha) of the township, which have been identified by field-walking. At a date still unknown, these were gathered into a single, compact community of 30 or so houses. The arrangement of these houses, so regularly along three frontages, and also the documentary evidence for a methodical distribution of land within the fields presupposes a major conscious act of planning. The period most favoured for this striking move, also matched locally in other Wolds villages, is currently that of the Scandinavian period (tenth century) although one piece of archaeological evidence (p. 78) stands in the way, pointing to the twelfth century. Thus, not all the questions that were in the mind in 1948 have been answered, and the research itself has prompted many others that were earlier unasked.

The investigation of the parish church demonstrated very well the way in which a combination of above-ground architectural survey with below-ground archaeological excavation reveals the complex development of the building in a way that would not have been possible from excavation alone.

Similarly, once the top levels of houses immediately beneath the visible earthworks were recovered others were revealed, but even these, in many cases, still proved not to be the first of the series. The sequence of houses progresses from timber to stone foundations, but their different alignments also warn that in every village with very clear earthworks visible by fieldwork or air photography the plan revealed is not of 'the' medieval village but only one of the latest of a series of medieval villages and layouts on that site. Had not the accident of desertion occurred evolution might well have continued, with considerable amounts of rebuilding to cope with new agricultural demands and practices. The layout of a present-day Wharram Percy might well not resemble that of the late-medieval earthworks.

Further back in time, from which house earthworks do not survive, methodical fieldwork, air photography, geophysical survey and limited excavations have given the area that was later to become two parishes and six villages a pre-medieval life. A careful excavation of one small area near Wharram Percy north manor house showed houses and the use of a trackway in every century for the last 2,000 years.

The excavation and the historical and other research conducted at Wharram Percy have acted as an exemplar well beyond Yorkshire,

for the last 40 years have seen the creation of the Deserted Medieval Village Research Group, the Moated Sites Research Group, the Society for Medieval Archaeology and its journal *Medieval Archaeology*. Wharram Percy happened to be an early, if not the first, English site of any archaeological period where excavation took the untraditional form of open-area excavation, so that (again as an exemplar) Wharram Percy influenced Deserted Medieval Village research excavations at Gomeldon, Wiltshire, Hound Tor, Devon, and Upton, Gloucestershire, and the extensive rescue excavation of a deserted medieval village at West Whelpington, Northumberland. This philosophy also spread to castle sites like Hen Domen and to urban sites like Winchester.

In the hands of others, just as the horizon of enquiry at Wharram Percy widened over this period, the same 40 years has seen the development of landscape history as an academic discipline, its concern being totality, just as at Wharram Percy the aim was to study the development of the site from prehistoric times to the present day; to set the visible remains in their chronological framework; and to extend research by the parish surveys, thus putting Wharram Percy in its context in time and place.

98 *The 1982 visit of the Ancient Monuments Board for England to inspect progress in presenting the site to the public, with Hurst making notes on the left.*

One of the fundamental points that 40 years work at Wharram Percy has shown is the danger of making wide-ranging conclusions from even quite large-area excavations. Each new site has tended to raise new questions as well as throwing into doubt many earlier suggestions.

The lesson for archaeology in general is that while on a moated or castle site, which is limited in area, it is practical to obtain the main story from a major excavation, a deserted medieval village, which may cover up to 40 acres, is so complex that the 6 per cent sample excavated at Wharram Percy is not sufficient to give a full and final explanation of the development of the site. This throws into doubt the interpretation of the many excavations where only a sample toft has been investigated: experience, even as long as 40 years, also teaches humility.

The last 40 years

In the 40 years of the excavation Time has not stood still: on the site in recent Julys one could encounter more than one grandchild of volunteers who had first met each other at the excavation. In these years, quite apart from the changes in the landscape engineered as part of English Heritage's plans for presentation of the site to the public, such as the ring fence, the new plantations and the pond, economic circumstances have brought transformations to the landscape just as they did in the past.

The railway trains, still running in 1949, have gone, and the bus from Malton to Wharram crossroads, once the main artery of communication, has become a collector's rarity. Wharram station is a private house, the railway track a private road. The tunnel entrance is bricked up and disappearing into a forest of undergrowth. Among the former sidings, which are grassed over and beginning to be colonized by cowslips, the great Wharram limestone quarry is a Nature Reserve and the kilns, crusher and hoppers are tumbling into ruins. The pump from the Malton waterworks that once punctuated the remote silence at Wharram Percy has been removed and its brick housing is disappearing from view behind a new plantation. On the hillside to the east the Nut Wood plantation, which was as young as the Milner children in 1949, is now middle aged. Beresford and Hurst are retired pensioners.

The schoolrooms at Wharram le Street, where the small band of volunteers slept for two weekends early in the history of the excavation, have long been closed and are now a village hall. At the crossroads nearby, where puzzled visitors, British and foreign, used to find that the misleading signpost to 'Wharram Percy' sent them to Wharram Percy Farm rather than to the excavation, an official sign now authenticates 'Wharram Percy Deserted Medieval Village' and points the visitor towards the car park alongside Bella Farm. As visitors descend the hollow way that was once the road along which coffins were led from Towthorpe for burial, a footbridge takes them for a moment into the overgrown disused railway cutting and then, as they follow the track towards the English Heritage 'Welcome' signboard, the earthworks of the village and the top of the church tower come into sight.

They see, among the ancient earthworks, the concrete signs and the fresh gravel rectangles that mark out where the labours of the last 40 years have uncovered peasant houses, the Norman manor house, the vicarages, the seventeenth-century farmstead, and its enlargement by an extended range of outbuildings. Doubtless another 40 years will see the saplings that have restored apples to the vicarage garden grow to be substantial trees, and the whole site will lie in the shade of the fine new hedgerows and plantations that have been set along the perimeter of the area that is in the care of English Heritage.

Further reading

The Wharram Research Project

The full results are in process of publication in a series of monographs published by the Society for Medieval Archaeology and the University of York, Department of Archaeology. Six have so far appeared. These are listed under the appropriate chapters. Full interim reports of some 30 typed pages have been issued each year. The main results are published in the *Annual Reports* of the Medieval Village Research Group (since 1986 the Medieval Settlement Research Group) while shorter reports appear each year in *Medieval Archaeology* and *Post-Medieval Archaeology*. Other reports, some general, some specialist, are listed in the monographs.

1 The Village site

A general introduction to deserted medieval villages is given in Maurice Beresford, *The Lost Villages of England* (Lutterworth, 1954; 2nd ed. 1983. Alan Sutton, Gloucester), written two years after the partnership at Wharram Percy had begun. This was brought up to date in 1968: M.W. Beresford and J.G. Hurst (eds.), *Deserted Medieval Villages: Studies* (Lutterworth 1971; 2nd ed. 1989, Alan Sutton, Gloucester) which includes an historical update, a summary of the archaeological evidence from medieval villages and a full bibliography, together with revised county lists of deserted villages. R. T. Rowley and J. Wood, *Deserted Villages* (Shire Publications, Princess Risborough, 1982) is a popular general account of the subject.

The historical background is covered in E. Miller and J. Hatcher, *Medieval England: rural society and economic change, 1086–1348* (Longman, 1978), the most informed available account of the period. J. Hatcher, *Plague, Population and the English Economy, 1348–1530* (Macmillan, 1977) is a brief but indispensable account of the period of rural contraction.

2 Early Excavations

For medieval archaeology in general there are two textbooks: J. M. Steane, *The Archaeology of Medieval England and Wales* (Croom Helm, 1984) and Helen Clarke, *The Archaeology of Medieval England* (British Museum Publications, 1984). The development of archaeological techniques is covered by P. Barker, *The Techniques of Archaeological Excavation* (Batsford, 1977).

The detailed results of the 1950s and 1960s excavations of the Area 10 and 6 peasant houses sites are given in the first monograph in the series *Wharram: A Study of Settlement on the Yorkshire Wolds;* D. D. Andrews and G. Milne (eds.), *Domestic Settlement 1: Areas 10 and 6* (Society for Medieval Archaeology Monograph Series 8, 1979). This has been brought up to date and re-interpreted in the sixth monograph: Stuart Wrathmell, *Domestic Settlement 2: Medieval Peasant Farmsteads* (York University Archaeological Publications 8, 1989).

A detailed reconstruction of a medieval village from historical documents can be found in P. D. A. Harvey, *A Medieval Oxfordshire Village, Cuxham, 1240–1400*, (Oxford University Press, 1965), and a series of popular reconstructions of medieval daily life in Sheila Sancha, *The Luttrell Village: Country Life in the Early Fourteenth Century* (William Collins, 1982).

Among other relevant excavation reports is D. Austin, *The Deserted Medieval Village of Thrislington County Durham Excavations 1973–1974* (Society for Medieval Archaeology Monograph Series 12, 1989), which describes a village with stone-built houses in the north. For sites on clay in the Midlands; see G. T. M. Beresford, *The Medieval Clay-land Village: Excavations at Goltho (Lincolnshire) and Barton Blount (Derbyshire)* (Society for Medieval Archaeology Monograph Series 6, 1975).

3 Official Recognition

Detailed results of the excavation of the parish church are given in the third Wharram monograph: R. D. Bell, M. W. Beresford *et al.*, *Wharram Percy: The Church of St Martin* (Society for Medieval Archaeology Monograph Series 11, 1987).

For preliminary results of the study of the burials, see D. Brothwell, 'British palaeodemography and earlier British populations', *World Archaeology*, 9, 1972, 75–87.

4 Wider Questions

A general account of the Wharram topography is given in J. G. Hurst, 'The Topography of Wharram Percy Village' in B. K. Roberts and R. E. Glasscock (eds.), *Villages, Fields and Frontiers: Studies in European Rural Settlement in the Medieval and Early Modern Periods* (British Archaeological Reports International Series 185, 1983, 3–20.

Village plans are dealt with in B. K. Roberts, *The Making of the English Village: A Study in Historical Geography* (Longman, 1987), and also in a more popular version: B. K. Roberts, *Village Plans* (Shire Publications, Princess Risborough, 1982).

5 A Further Horizon

The pioneer study in landscape archaeology is W. G. Hoskins, *The Making of the English Landscape* (Hodder & Stoughton, 1955), reprinted with introduction and commentary by C. C. Taylor, 1988.

Three recent books summarize the major advances in the study of the landscape and its interpretation over the last 20 years: C. C. Taylor, *Village and Farmstead: A History of Rural Settlement in England* (George Philip, 1983), M. Aston, *Interpreting the Landscape: Landscape Archaeology in Local Studies* (Batsford, 1985), and M. Aston, D. Austin and C. Dyer (eds.) *The Rural Settlements of Medieval England: Studies Dedicated to Maurice Beresford and John Hurst* (Blackwell, 1989).

An account of the Wharram parishes survey, mainly dealing with the Iron Age and Roman periods, is given in the fifth Wharram monograph by C. Hayfield, *An Archaeological Survey of the Parish of Wharram Percy, East Yorkshire: 1. The Evolution of the Roman Landscape* (British Archaeological Reports British Series 172, 1987). A detailed account of the trial exca-

vations on the two Wharram Roman villas forms the third Wharram monograph: P. Rahtz, C. Hayfield and J. Bateman, *Two Roman Villas at Wharram le Street* (York University Archaeological Publications 2, 1986).

Archaeological fieldwork, including the techniques used at Wharram is included in C. Hayfield (ed.), *Fieldwalking as a Method of Archaeological Research* (Directorate of Ancient Monuments, Department of the Environment, Occasional Paper no. 2, 1980).

For more general surveys, see C. Taylor, *Fieldwork in Medieval Archaeology* (Batsford, 1974) and A. Brown, *Fieldwork for Archaeologists and Local Historians* (Batsford, 1987).

General accounts of air photography can be found in D. R. Wilson, *Air Photo Interpretation for Archaeologists* (Batsford, 1982) and in D. N. Riley, *Air Photography and Archaeology* (Duckworth, 1987). For the medieval period specifically, M.W. Beresford & J.K.S. St. Joseph, *Medieval England: An Aerial Survey* (Cambridge University Press, 1958; 2nd ed. 1979) forms a good background.

The first coherent account of the topography of open field farming, especially that surviving at Laxton, Notts., is to be found in C. S. and C. S. Orwin, *The Open Fields* (Clarendon Press, Oxford, 1938; 3rd ed. 1967). The third edition has an extended preface by Dr Joan Thirsk. A. R. H. Baker and R. A. Butlin (eds.), *Studies of Field Systems in the British Isles* (Cambridge University Press, 1973), offers a series of region-by-region studies; June Sheppard (Ch. 4) is concerned with Yorkshire, and with regular field systems there, while Chapter 14 by the editors is a general survey. For a collection of essays on the same subject, see Trevor Rowley (ed.), *The Origins of Open Field Agriculture* (Croom Helm, 1981); especially relevant are Chapter 2 by David Hall and Chapter 9 by Mary Harvey. A more popular account, including reference to Wharram, is given in D. Hall, *Medieval Fields* (Shire Publications, Princess Risborough, 1982).

6 The Site after Desertion

Old photographs of Wharram and neighbouring villages are collected in C. Hayfield, *Birdsall Estate Remembered* and *Thixendale Remembered* (Kingate Press, Birmingham, 1988). For the later burials, see the second Wharram monograph by P. Rahtz and L. Watts, *Wharram Percy: the memorial stones of the churchyard*

(York University Archaeological Publications 1, 1983). The only serious study of the age of agricultural improvement in the Wolds and in other parts of the county, illustrated by many maps, is by A. Harris, *The Rural Landscape of the East Riding of Yorkshire, 1750–1850* (Oxford University Press, 1961).

7 A Site for the Public

English Heritage Education booklet for the site: M. Atkin and K. Tompkins, *Revealing Lost Villages: Wharram Percy* (English Heritage, 1986).

A general background to ecology can be found in O. Rackham, *The History of the Countryside* (Dent, 1986) and for the Wharram area in particular, C. J. Smith. *The Ecology of the English Chalk* (Academic Press, 1980).

8 Forty Years in the Field

There are two comparable research publications, documenting over 40 years' work: C. J. Atkinson, *Forty Years in a Moorland Parish* (Macmillan, 1891) – a summary by J. G. O'Leary, *Countryman on the Moors*, was published by MacGibbon & Kee (1967) and reissued as an Oxford University Press paperback in 1983. The second is J. R. Mortimer, *Forty Years' Researches in British and Saxon Burial Mounds of East Yorkshire* (Brown, London, 1905).

Other sites to visit

Besides Wharram Percy, there are two other Deserted Medieval Villages in the care of English Heritage: Gainsthorpe in South Humberside, and Hound Tor in Devonshire, both of which are good quality sites with the earthworks of stone-built houses.

Location of finds

The objects found on the Wharram Percy excavations are being deposited in Hull City Museum as reports are published. These are available for study, and examples are on display from time to time. The Malton Museum in North Yorkshire also holds occasional Wharram exhibitions.

Glossary

Many of the words given have various meanings. In this glossary the meaning applicable to Wharram Percy has been used and, where possible, attention is drawn to illustrations of the term.

Advowson   The right to present (nominate) the incumbent of a church.

Air photography   Earthwork sites are often much clearer from the air than from the ground and may be observed as parchmarks or shadows. If a site has been ploughed flat then the site may appear as crop- or soilmarks.

Cropmarks   Areas of differential colouring in growing crops. The soil now filling buried ditches and pits allows more luxuriant growth than the shallow soil over the natural chalk and under damp conditions. This shows up as dark marks as the cereal crop begin to ripen and turn yellow (**65b**).

Parchmarks   Where building were constructed of stone the wall foundations, which are near the surface with a thin covering of turf, cause the grass in a dry season to turn brown, while the grass around with a deeper soil covering remains green. In a black and white air photo the parchmarks show as light lines, as may be seen in **7** and **51**.

Soilmarks   When an earthwork site is ploughed and levelled, soils of different colours are brought to the surface. In **6** the ridge and furrow is visible as surviving earthworks. By the time that **32** was taken the field had been ploughed. The ridges show up as light marks because of the chalky soil, while the furrows are dark because of the depth of plough soil.

Amphora   A large two-handled storage vessel usually used in the Roman period for the importation of wine and oil from the Mediterranean.

Apse   a semi-circular east end to a chancel, as in **41** and **44**.

Ashlar   Squared blocks of stone worked to an even face, and laid in regular courses with fine joints, as opposed to rubble or unworked stone straight from a quarry.

Baffle entrance   A doorway into a house after which it is not possible to go straight into a room as the way is blocked by a wall, usually containing a chimney stack, so that it is necessary to turn either left or right into the rooms on either side. See **78**.

Baulk   An unexcavated strip left between two excavated areas. The two baulks left in Area 10 may be clearly seen in **19**.

Borre   A Scandinavian art style named from objects found in the ship burial in a great barrow at Borre in Vestfold in Norway and datable to the late ninth and early tenth centuries. It is most commonly found on small cast copper-alloy objects like the Wharram example and is typified by a ring chain pattern made up of a double ribbon plait forming a symmetrical interlace. Each intersection is bound by a circle which surrounds a hollow-sided lozenge. Borre-style objects were not necessarily imported and were made in the north of England, for example at York. See **colour plate 5**.

Bovate   Originally as much land as an ox could plough in a year: hence often called oxgang; later, a unit holding of arable land lying in the open fields together with rights in the common pasture and meadow. (Also, in Domesday Book a fraction of a **carucate**.)

Brick Bonds
English bond (**99**) in which the bricks are laid in alternate courses of stretchers (with the long sides visible) and headers (with the short ends visible), so that each alternate course is bonded through. This is the common European medieval bond which was used

99 *English bond brickwork.*

again in the north of England in the nineteenth century, particularly after the coming of the railways.

English garden-wall bond (**100**) in which there is a single course of headers and then five (or sometimes three) courses of stretchers. This is not so strong since the bricks are bonded only through every fourth or sixth course. This is the characteristic post-medieval bond in the north of England for ordinary buildings.

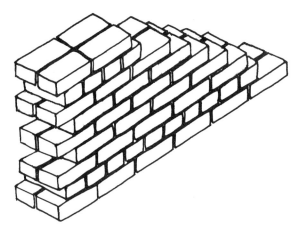

100 *English garden-wall bond brickwork.*

Bullace A small tree or large shrub bearing black fruits 1–1½ in. (2–3 cm) long with comparatively large stones. Spreads by suckers – shoots arising from underground from parts of the root system – and therefore often develops into dense stands. Frequently found near to former habitation; not much grown today. Technically a sub species of the plum and its allies; the normal plum of gardens is another sub species.

Cartulary The record of a landowner's (usually monastic) possessions in book form.

Carucate A unit of valuation in Domesday Book, notionally based on capacity for a plough team.

Chantry An endowment, usually of land, the income from which would ensure masses for the souls of the donor and his family at an altar in the parish church or in a chapel.

Coppice The system of repeatedly cutting back a woody plant every 6–20 years. The part which remains permanently is the coppice stool. From this coppice stool grow poles, from between about three and eight in number. These economic poles are the product, and are used for fencing, simple furniture, small timber for building, tool handles etc.

Croft An enclosed piece of land adjoining a village house.

Cruck A pair of large curved timbers used as the principal support for the roof of a building. The walls are added but are not load-bearing. The method of construction may be seen in **23**, **26** and **76**.

Dais Raised platform at the upper end of a manorial hall for a high table for the lord. This may be seen in plan on **8** and in the reconstructed drawing (**colour plate 9**).

Demesne The portion of a village's fields worked by or for the lord of the manor.

Dower The rights of a widow during her lifetime to a portion (often one-third) of her late husband's estate.

Faculty Authority to carry out works in and around a church.

Family monastery An irregular Saxon monastery set up by noble families for their own purposes and not following the strict Benedictine rules.

Farm In the Iron Age and Roman periods a lower status site than the Roman **villa** with simple timber buildings, not stone-built but sometimes with tiled roofs. It is less artefact-rich, with a wide range of local and imported pottery types but no Mediterranean amphorae.

Fauna The complete range of different types of animals found in one location.

Flora The complete range of different types of plants found at one location. See also **Fauna**.

Furlong (or **Flatt**) A sub-division of the arable open fields, within which the constituent selions (below) had their long axes parallel, as in **74**.

Garderobe A lavatory in the thickness of the wall of a building with a chute leading down to a pit in the ground.

Garrett Room within the roof of a house; an attic.

Garth A small piece of enclosed land next to a house, often a garden.

Geophysical survey A magnetometer which measures the changes in the magnetism of the earth's surface is moved over the ground. It picks up anomalies and can therefore detect the presence of ditches and pits which are filled with loser soil than the solid chalk that they are cut into. The Wharram results, very similar to cropmarks (above), are seen on **52** and **64**.

Glebe Land belonging to the parish church.

Green An area of common grassland within a village used for grazing; at Wharram the central sloping area between the three Rows of houses (**34**).

Grubenhaus (plural *Grubenhäuser*) A small hut dug into the ground, usually with a post hole at each end, typical of the Saxon period. It is debatable whether they were flimsy buildings with floors at the lower level, or whether they were more substantial structures with raised wooden floors and a cavity underneath. They have been given various names, such as sunken hut, sunken-feature building but the latter is very confusing a it is often confused with sunken-floored building. It is preferable to retain the neutral German term for this type of structure (**58**)

Hurdle A portable rectangular wooden frame, strengthened with **wattles**, and used at Wharram to strengthen the mill dam.

Improving Forms of husbandry replacing or modifying the practices of open field farming to increase efficiency or yields.

Infield-outfield A system of cultivation where an infield, usually near to the village, was cropped and manured continuously while the much larger outfield was divided into portions which were cropped only at intervals.

Isometric A geometric projection to show a building in three dimensions, and from which correct measurements can be taken in any direction. See **49**, **90** and **93**.

Ladder In the Iron Age and Roman periods a number of rectangular ditched enclosures placed in line to form a pattern like a ladder. Best seen on **65** in the Gypsey Race ladder. See also **Row**.

Living The ecclesiastical benefice of a rector or vicar.

Long-house A building in which both humans and animal live under the same roof. It comprises a living room with a central hearth and an inner room for sleeping or dairying, sometimes with a storage loft above. There is a cross-passage with opposing doors separating the living part from the animals. Sometimes there is no evidence for animals and the third room is likely to have been for various types of farm storage. See plan and reconstruction **23** and **26**.

Lynchet A bank formed by ploughing for a long period on a slope where a field has a fixed boundary, such as hedge or fence. On the upper side, soil moves down to form a positive lynchet against the boundary while below it the soil is cut away to form a negative lynchet.

Open-area excavation In which the whole area to be investigated is opened up at once without **baulks**. The site is excavated layer by layer and recorded so that each feature is seen to its fullest extent without hindrance, and sections can be constructed at any significant point required.

Open fields Arable land with common rights after harvest or while fallow. Usually without internal divisions by hedges, walls or fences but made up of **selions** arranged by **furlongs**.

Padstone A large flat-topped stone on which a timber upright or cruck could be placed instead of putting the post directly in to the ground.

Pantile Roofing tile of curved S-shaped section.

Parsonage The house occupied by a rector (rectory) or vicar (vicarage).

Pentice A covered way with open sides to enable people to walk between separate buildings in the dry when it is raining, for example at Wharram Percy between the detached kitchen and the hall at the north manor, shown on **8**.

Plurality Incumbent holding more than one benefice at the same time.

Radiocarbon dating A scientific method of dating those archaeological objects which were once alive. Carbon 14 is a radioactive isotope. When living matter dies no further carbon is taken in and the radioactive carbon begins to decay. By measuring the amount of radioactive carbon remaining in the object, the age of the material can be assessed.

Rector Incumbent whose tithes have not been alienated; see **Tithes**.

Ridge-and-furrow Parallel bands of elevated ridges and depressed furrows created by ploughing the **selion** between the same limits year after year; except as soil- or cropmarks now usually visible only in land converted to pasture.

Row A morphologically distinct unit, in which the homesteads, tofts and crofts, are arranged in a regular line (**34**). At Wharram this is the medieval equivalent of the Iron Age and Roman ladder patterns.

Scandinavian period Between the middle of the ninth century when the Vikings, mainly from Denmark, invaded and settled in eastern England, till the Norman conquest in 1066. It was a time of strong Scandinavian influence with major changes in land ownership in the Wharram area as Viking lords took over Saxon estates and often renamed them. This was the time of Jorvik, the Viking kingdom at York.

Sceat (plural Sceattas) A Saxon silver coin of the late seventh, eighth and early ninth centuries.

Selion The smallest operational unit for ploughing within the open arable fields; the bounds of each were well known, with stones or other markers. The shape was long and narrow, with several selions to the acre: confusingly, selions were often called acres, as in **74**.

Sheep A Ewe is a female sheep, a Hogget a yearling sheep and a Wether a male sheep, especially a castrated ram.

Shrunken In respect of a settlement, where previous house-sites are now unoccupied but often visible as earthworks, cropmarks or soil-marks.

Smithy A blacksmith's workshop where iron objects are forged as opposed to a smelting workshop where iron is extracted from the ore.

Solar An upper private living room in a manor house. Usually on the first floor but at Wharram Percy, as the undercroft was a cellar, it was at ground level.

Solskift From the Scandinavian terms for 'sun-division', an arrangement of holdings such that the order of houses along the village street(s) matched that of the householders' selions within each furlong of the open fields, as in **74**.

Standards Trees that are allowed to grow up to full size before being harvested. In the medieval period a wood would consist of a mixture of **coppice** and standards. Viewed from above, about 70 per cent of the land surface would be coppice, and about 30 per cent standards.

Styca A Saxon copper coin of the ninth century.

Tating ware A type of hard wheel-thrown grey pottery pitcher, decorated with applied strips of tin foil, made in the Rhineland and northern France in the late eighth and early ninth centuries. Found in England only at the main trading centres and important royal or religious centres.

Terrier A written description of a property.

Tithe The proportion (originally a tenth) of produce paid to an incumbent: if a vicar had been instituted he took only the 'small' tithes, and the rector the remainder.

Toft The place where a house stood or had once stood; usually adjoining a **croft** or **garth**.

Undercroft A lower room, either at ground level or underground, often used for storage, beneath a principal room (the **Solar**).

Vicar An incumbent acting for the rector and not receiving the full tithes.

Villa A settlement of the Roman period which shows high status as the buildings were of stone, had tiled roofs, polychrome mosaic floors and decorated polychrome painted plaster on their walls. It was also artefact-rich with good quality pottery including Mediterranean amphorae. See also **Farm**.

Villein An occupier entirely subject to a manorial lord, as opposed to a free tenant.

Voussoirs Wedge-shaped stones which, placed together form an arch.

Warren An area reserved for the rearing of rabbits.

Wattle A wooden frame with spaced vertical rods with horizontal rods woven between alternate ways, used for hurdles, fences, or walls and as a revetment for the mill dam at Wharram.

Index